POO THROUGH THE AGES

SUZIE EDGE

To Mrs Fenby's and Miss Ramli's Year 3 class of 2022–23 at Terrington Hall School, North Yorkshire

and for

Niki Daines,
still trying to make you laugh mate.

First published in Great Britain in 2024 by Wren & Rook

Text copyright © Suzie Edge 2024
Illustrations copyright © Luke Newell 2024
All rights reserved.

The right of Suzie Edge and Luke Newell to be identified as the author and illustrator respectively of this Work has been asserted by them in accordance with the Copyright, Designs & Patents Act 1988

ISBN: 978 1 5263 6655 9

1 3 5 7 9 10 8 6 4 2

MIX
Paper | Supporting responsible forestry
FSC® C104740

Wren & Rook
An imprint of
Hachette Children's Group
Part of Hodder & Stoughton
Carmelite House
50 Victoria Embankment
London EC4Y 0DZ

An Hachette UK Company
www.hachette.co.uk
www.hachettechildrens.co.uk

Printed and bound in Great Britain by Clays Ltd, Elcograf S.p.A.

HISTORY STINKS

POO THROUGH THE AGES

SUZIE EDGE

ILLUSTRATED BY
LUKE NEWELL

CONTENTS

INTRODUCTION   7

CHAPTER ONE: Roman Rears and Toilet Troubles   13

CHAPTER TWO: Around the World in Ancient Toilets   29

CHAPTER THREE: The Viking and the GIANT Poo   45

CHAPTER FOUR: Old Medicine for Pooey Problems   59

CHAPTER FIVE: Medieval Muck   69

CHAPTER SIX: Tudor Number Twos   **87**

CHAPTER SEVEN: A Royal Flush and DYING for the Loo   **101**

CHAPTER EIGHT: Victorian Whiffs   **113**

CHAPTER NINE: Beastly Bacteria   **127**

CHAPTER TEN: Poo at War!   **137**

CHAPTER ELEVEN: Poo Discoveries   **151**

CHAPTER TWELVE: Poo in Space — and Beyond!   **165**

POO QUIZ   **181**

GLOSSARY   **188**

INTRODUCTION

This book is full of poo, and guess what? It stinks! (The poo, I mean, not the book. Unless something has gone very wrong at your local bookshop.)

But why on earth would anyone want to read a book that's full of poo, I hear you ask? Well, if you hold your nose and ignore the smell, poo can teach you a lot. Humans poo every day – and we've done so throughout our history – so there's plenty of it sloshing about in the murkiest corners of our past. The story of how we've dealt with poo through the ages – from the foul-smelling ancient Romans to the whiffy Vikings to pongy present-day folk – can tell us all about how we once lived.

You also might be wondering: **why does this author love talking about poo so much?** It's a fair question! Well, as a medical doctor, I'm interested in human bodies and have known about the importance of poo health for years. **I also love history.** Poo can tell us so much about our ancestors and how they looked after their bodies as well as how they built their homes and cities. **So for me, poo plus history is the perfect combination!**

DID YOU KNOW?

Just in case you were wondering what exactly poo is – it's what's left over after the process of digestion, which is your body's way of breaking down food and giving you the energy you need to live. Poo is mostly made up of water, but it also contains all those bits of food your body hasn't quite managed to absorb, as well as dead blood cells, which give it its famous brown colour.

And why does it smell? Well, that comes from bacteria that break down food during digestion. Thanks, bacteria!

Poo has many different names, from poops and plops to dung and doo-doo. But no matter what it's called, we have always had to get rid of it. Poo can spread diseases, and it doesn't matter who you are – humble servant or legendary king or queen – anyone can get sick from poo. It has caused all sorts of trouble in places where people have lived close together, from the busiest cities to army camps, to ships belonging to famous explorers and even outer space. **Pesky poo gets everywhere!**

So, it's about time we lift the (toilet) lid on the stinkiest, pongiest, smelliest and grossest corners of humanity's poo-tastic history, and ask the biggest, ploppiest questions you all want answered, such as: How many Romans did it take to do a poo together? What did the Tudors use to wipe their bums? How did people in medieval times get rid of their muck?

AND MUCH MORE.

We will even learn how our ancestors used poo for good and discover how looking after our poo could help us look after the planet in the future. Now, there's no more holding it in, it's time to grab some loo roll – and possibly a peg for your nose – **WE'RE GOING IN!**

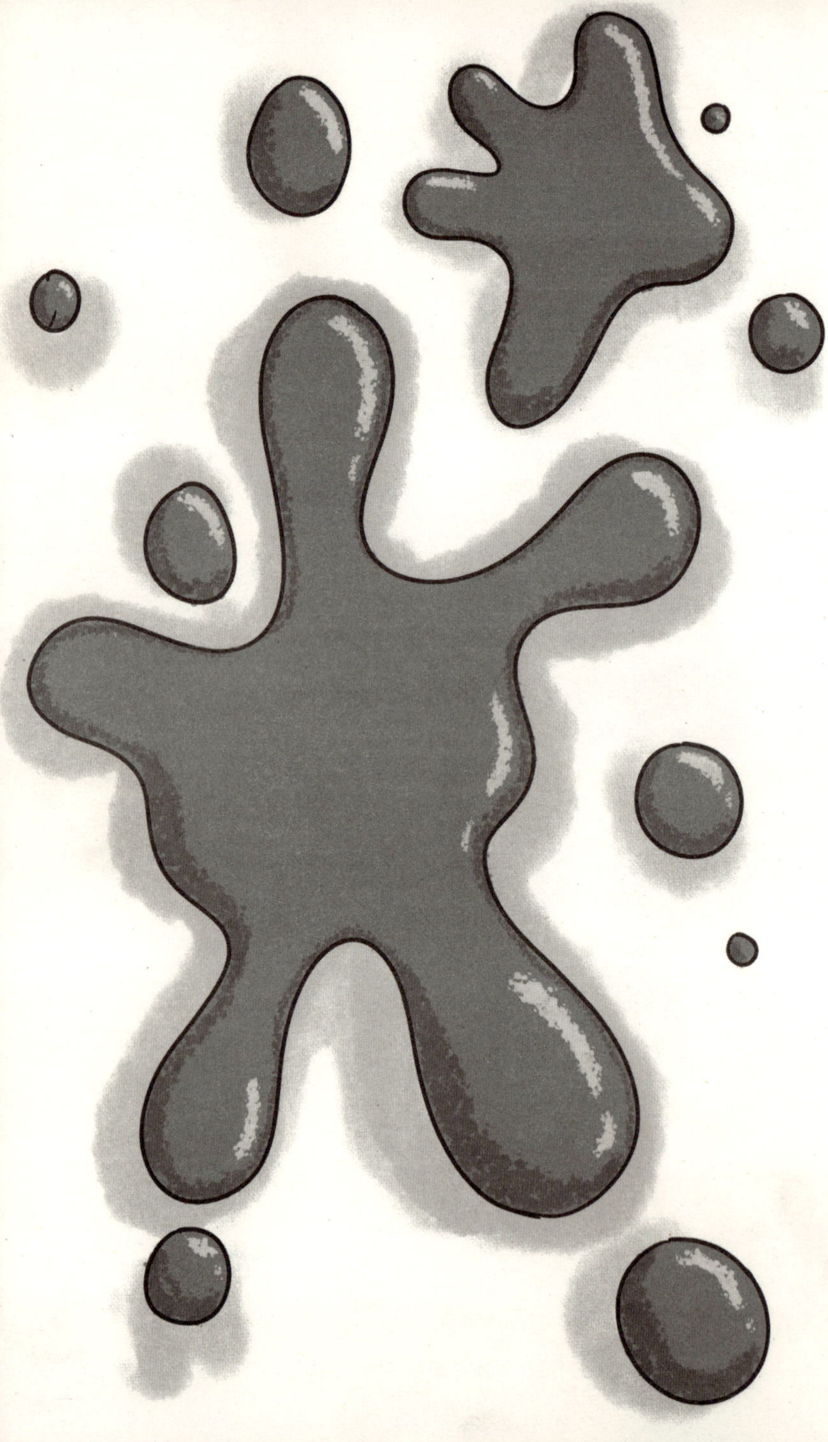

CHAPTER ONE: ROMAN REARS AND TOILET TROUBLES

Friends, Romans, countrymen, lend me your bottom brush! We're all going to the toilet together in ancient Rome. Everything you've ever wanted to know about Romans and their pooing and farting habits is here. I would hold my nose if I were you – there is a serious **STINKUS MAXIMUS** about the place! Oh, and if you don't have a bottom brush to lend me, then don't worry, I'm sure there'll be one lying around somewhere. (And if you don't know what one of those is, all will be revealed!)

EMPEROR CLAUDIUS AND THE TRAPPED WIND

Before we empty our bowels, let's set the scene. The Roman Empire was an ancient state that had control over most of the people in Europe, the north of Africa and the west of Asia, from the first to the fifth centuries CE.* **It was truly MASSIVE!**

The empire was ruled by mighty emperors, one of whom was Claudius, who was the fourth to take charge, way back in 41 CE. Clever Claudius was known for building giant aqueducts – huge structures that moved water from the hills to the cities – as well as canals that helped move people and goods around.

All pretty impressive stuff, right? RIGHT! But even emperors have to deal with pesky bum trouble every now and then. For instance, one time Claudius held a lavish feast to celebrate all the building work that had

*CE stands for COMMON ERA, and is an alternative to AD (ANNO DOMINI).

been going on in his empire. All was going fantastically well – the meat and fish were delicious and the wine was top notch! (What else would you expect when you're dining with an emperor?)

However, one of the guests, a senator, had a little bit of a problem. All that fancy food had made him *desperate* to pass wind, but he couldn't possibly risk offending the emperor by making a noise or a nasty smell. So instead of letting it out, he simply held it in. As you know, that's never a good idea. Gases starting building and building inside him until he nearly popped like a

GIANT, SMELLY BALLOON!

The emperor Claudius heard the commotion the senator was making and when he was told what was happening, announced that he would allow the passing of wind at the dinner table to ease the pressure. **PHEW!** Everyone was very relieved and they all relaxed. What a noise – and smell – they must have made!

> **DISCLAIMER: I CAN'T GUARANTEE THIS STORY WILL LET YOU OFF THE HOOK IF YOU DECIDE TO PASS WIND AT YOUR DINNER TABLE!**

WHERE WOULD YOU GO TO POO IN ANCIENT ROME?

But what if the senator needed to do more than just pass wind? What if he needed a POO? It was all right for Claudius – he would have had his own private latrine to visit, but not everyone had that luxury. It sounds a bit weird to us, but the senator might have had to go with other ancient Romans, in public toilets called **foricae**.

Foricae were long, rectangular rooms built alongside public baths. They had benches running around three of the walls (shown below), set over trenches of running water. Holes were cut out on the top of the benches for people to sit over and, well, let it *all* out.

PLOP!

On a cold day you might have wanted to pay someone to sit there for a while to warm it up before you needed to go. (Although, maybe the thought of someone else's bum cheeks warming up the toilet is not that appealing to you, which is fair enough!) There were no cubicles in the **foricae** and very little privacy – unless you were wearing a large toga or tunic you could wrap around yourself. Some **foricae** could have held more than twenty people all going at the same time, but one of the biggest, in Julius Caesar's forum, could hold fifty. That's a serious amount of public pooers!

QUICK QUESTION

If you had to sit next to someone on the toilet, what would you say to break the tension? Perhaps you could tell a joke:

What did the poo say to the fart?
You BLOW me away!

THE CLEANING SPONGE
(IT'S AS DISGUSTING AS IT SOUNDS)

The holes in the **foricae** weren't just for people to sit over – they also extended down the front, so that you could reach under and, well, **wipe your bum!** Instead of loo roll – which they hadn't got round to inventing – ancient Romans used a special stick with a sponge on the end. (I told you we would talk about bum brushes!) The stick was called a **xylospongium** or a **tersorium**, which means **'the wiping thing'**. (I hope the sponge never fell off the stick while you were wiping . . . ouch!)

MMM, DELICIOUS!

You would find the **tersorium** in a bucket filled with vinegar or soured wine in the middle of the room. When you were done cleaning, you would rinse the sponge in the channel of cleaner water that ran in front of the benches and put it back in the bucket for whoever needed to use it next.

WHAT'S BROWN AND STICKY?

A STICK!

It can't have been that easy to wash the poo off the **tersorium – anything left behind such as bacteria or parasites might easily jump from bum to bum.** So, it was probably best not to look too closely at what might be sticking to the bum brush!

Things weren't quite as clean in the public toilets as the farting senator might have hoped. They were dark, dirty, dung-filled places, full of rats and snakes that loved to hang out there amongst all the stinking waste.

WHAT A PLACE TO PLOP!

JUST WHAT HAPPENED TO ALL THAT POO?

Outside, the Roman city streets were covered with animal dung and wee, all kinds of rubbish and lots of stagnant, filthy water. There was human poo and pee too, because poorer Romans had no toilets in their homes. Instead, they would empty chamber pots in public places or even poo in street corners (we'll hear more about chamber pots in chapter six). Houses and shops would have had an enormous load of waste and there would have been lots of flies buzzing about, sampling the goods. **Imagine the stench!**

> **WHAT DOES A FLY CALL POO? DINNER!**

But even though they were a bit grim, public toilets would have at least helped to reduce some of this mountain of muck. They would often be paid for by the rich, who preferred not to be stepping over and sliding about on so much poo in the streets. I can't blame them – **who wants to dodge a poo every time they go for a walk? Not me!**

A little before 500 BCE, the Etruscans, who were the people who lived in the cities of Etruria in ancient Italy, laid the first underground tunnels in the city of Rome. When the Romans came along, they used the tunnels to flush away the waste they made – handy, eh?

The biggest of the sewers in Rome was called The **Cloaca Maxima**. As well as washing away **HUGE** amounts of waste, it also helped prevent flooding, by emptying excess water into the River Tiber. The Cloaca Maxima was named after Cloacina, a Roman goddess whose name comes from the word 'clean' or 'purify'. I'd feel a bit miffed if I was that goddess – **all that mighty power and humans name a stinking sewer after you!**

DID YOU KNOW?

In 100 CE, the city of Rome boasted a million inhabitants. It's estimated they were producing around 90,000 kg of poo every couple of days – which is roughly equivalent to the weight of a blue whale!

IT'S A TOUGH JOB, BUT SOMEONE'S GOT TO DO IT!

With all that poo sloshing about, every so often the Roman toilets and sewers would need cleaning. Cleaners, who were most likely slaves or prisoners, would have to go down there with shovels and brushes to clean away the poo that was stuck to the sides and floors. You know, the ones that didn't flush away properly. **BARF!** What a job!

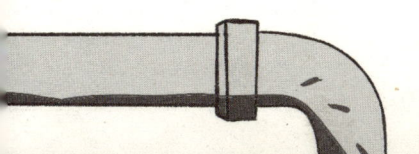

In toilets without running water underneath, poo would simply drop into a big pit. When that happened, someone had the job of getting it all out and carting it away. These lucky people were called **stercorarii**. They would have to take the poo to use it as a fertiliser, spreading it over gardens and fields to help crops grow. We can still see the remains of many Roman public toilets and sewer systems today. They can be found all over the former Roman Empire, from Rome in Italy to the north of England. Say what you want about those ancient Romans, but you can't deny they were big on poo!

EXPLODING TOILETS
(YES, YOU HEARD, EXPLODING TOILETS)

One thing Romans needed to watch out for was exploding toilets. Rotting poo gives off hydrogen sulphide and methane, both of which are highly flammable gases. If there was a spark, then the noxious, stinking gases could ignite and there could be a massive POO EXPLOSION!

PRRRRP!

With the help of the **stercorarii** and the running water underneath the **foricae**, they could get rid of the poo rather than just let it sit waiting to blow. Poo generally ended up in the River Tiber, which wasn't ideal, as people used the river as a water supply and to wash.

QUICK QUESTION

When you went for a bath in the river, you might have seen your own poo go floating by. Do you think you would recognise yours? Is your poo:

Curly?

Straight?

Zig-zag? (In which case, you might want to see someone about that!)

THE HUNGRY OCTOPUS

It was good for Romans to have sewer systems that linked toilets and houses to the waterways, but sometimes it was good for other creatures, too. Whilst poo went one way, sometimes animals could come up the other.

In the ancient city of Puteoli, there was a large house owned by a wealthy merchant. At night, when everything was quiet and the family were asleep in their beds, a **GIANT OCTOPUS** would sneak along the sewer, up through the hole in the toilet and into the house, where it would slither its way to the kitchen and help itself to the pickled fish stored there.

The family's servants would try and fight off the invader but it was too quick for them, diving back down into the sewers with a belly full of stolen fish. I hope it kept an eye out for any poop dropping on its head if anyone needed to use the toilet while it was there!

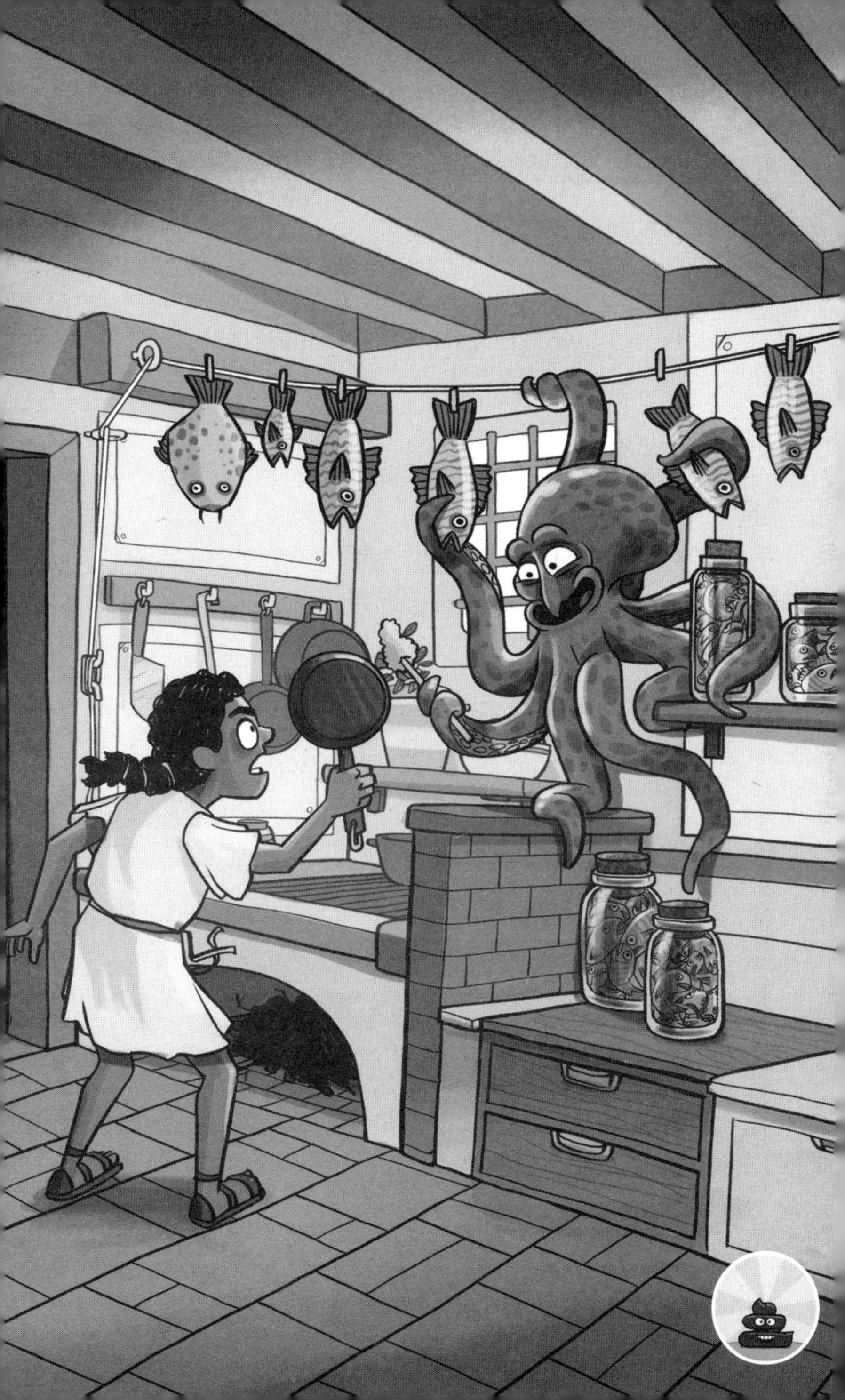

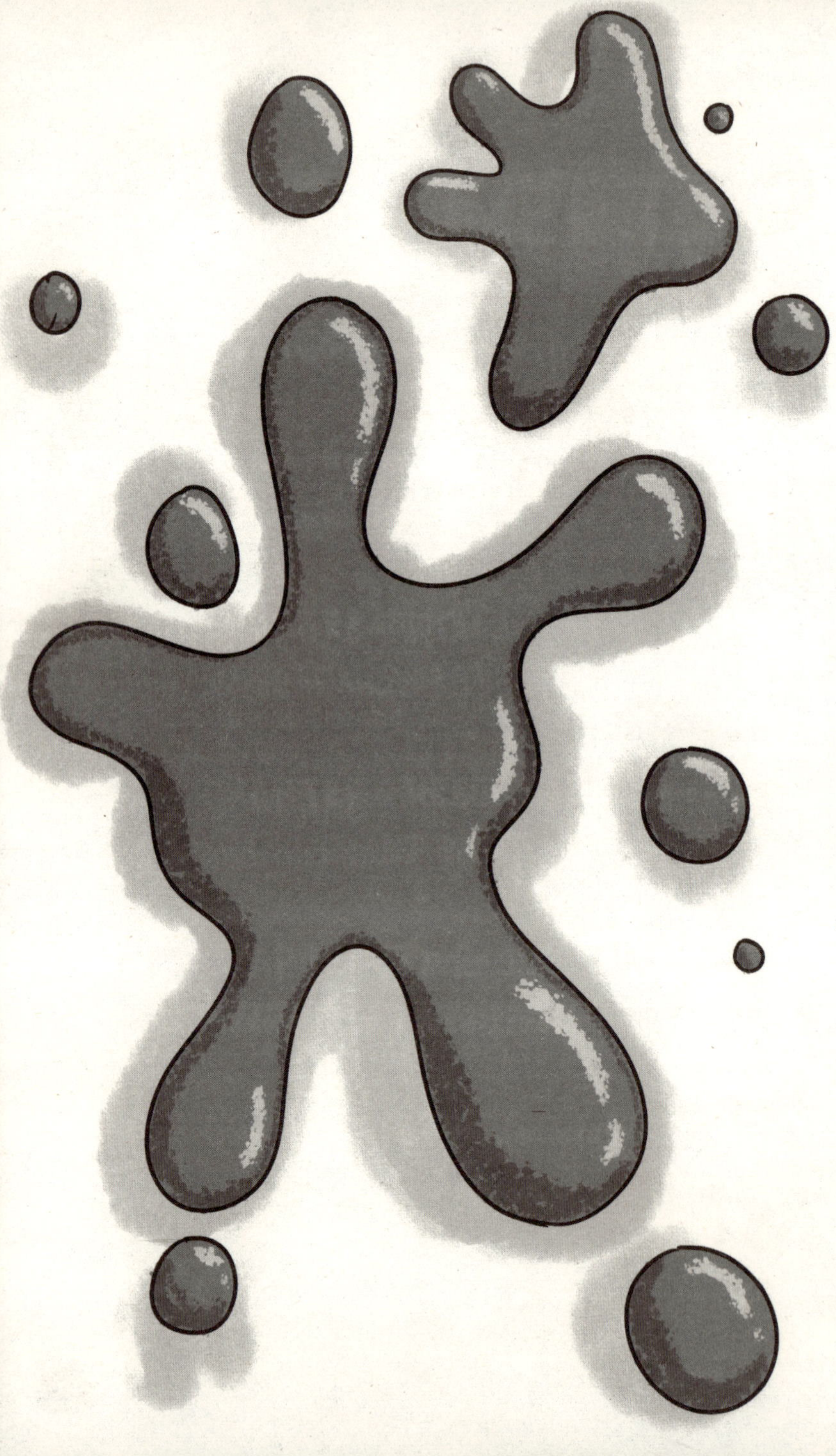

CHAPTER TWO: AROUND THE WORLD IN ANCIENT TOILETS

It wasn't just the ancient Romans who enjoyed a good poo. All around the world, evidence has been found of places where peoples of the past used to do their business. It's no surprise, really. **After all, everyone needs to go!** There are some very old toilets out there and lots of different countries like to claim they have the earliest ones ever. What a thing to be proud of! Let's go on an **EPIC journey** around the world *and* through time, to discover the terrific toilets of the past!

ANCIENT JAPAN

In Japan, although there are remains of toilets dating from 5,500 years ago, the oldest complete surviving one is a fourteenth-century structure at Tōfukuji, a temple in Kyoto. It's known as a **tosū**, and it resembles the ancient Roman **foricae**, though it's a bit more primitive. It was used by monks and is so vast that some people call it the hundred-person toilet. Imagine the smelly funk a hundred monks could make in that!

MESOPOTAMIA

Mesopotamia is an ancient region that sits between the Tigris and the Euphrates rivers, and now forms parts of Iraq, Turkey, Iran and Syria. Ceramic pots have been found there that were once used as squat toilets way back around **5,000 years ago**! (DON'T GET ANY IDEAS - YOUR PARENTS' PLANT POTS ARE NOT TO BE USED TO POO IN!)

> WAS THAT YOU? IT STINKS!

One of the world's oldest toilets you could actually sit on properly was found there, excavated in the city of Tell Asmar in Iraq. **It's over 4,000 years old!** Tell Asmar is also home to a hoard of famous artefacts depicting human worshippers of ancient gods – they have distinctive giant eyes made out of shells.

ANCIENT EGYPT

Ancient Egypt is not really remembered for having great toilets. Back in 3000 BCE, Egyptians with lots of money would have been able to pay other people to take buckets of poo away and empty their loos, but poorer Egyptians would have had to get rid of it themselves. And unfortunately, they didn't have sewers in ancient Egypt, so the poo was simply thrown into the River Nile or left to rot on the street. **Lovely, eh?**

Queen Cleopatra is a different story. This legendary queen, who ruled Egypt from 51 to 30 BCE, would have had proper toilets in her palaces, with seats made of limestone. Under the seat would have been a bowl filled with sand to catch the plops, which would be taken away by servants. Among the many things Cleopatra *is* remembered for is her bathroom habits. **She was said to have bathed in the milk from 700 donkeys. EACH TO THEIR OWN, I GUESS!**

THE HARAPPAN, INDUS VALLEY CIVILISATION, PAKISTAN AND INDIA

Along the Indus River Valley in present-day East Pakistan and Northern India we can see the earliest-known toilets and drains, dating all the way back to 2500 BCE. This period of time was called the Bronze Age (from 3300 BCE to 1200 BCE) because it came third after the Gold and Silver Ages in a race – **wait, no, that's not it at all!** It was called the Bronze Age because people who lived at that time used bronze to make tools for farming and weaponry.

When they weren't busy tilling the fields and fighting off their mortal enemies, they were building drains. The drainage systems of the Harappan civilisations were more cutting-edge than other sites from the same era. Most of their houses were made of mud bricks, built around courtyards. The courtyard buildings had platforms with holes in for people to do their **Bronze Age bum explosions**, the results of which went through clay pipes and down into cesspits.

A cesspit is a hole in the ground that is dug out to collect the piles of poo. From now on you will need to watch your step – we will come across a few cesspits in these stories. **Sometimes people fall into them and don't make it out alive!**

DID YOU KNOW?

'Gongfermors' or 'gong farmers' is a term to describe people whose job it was to clean out cesspits. It originates from Tudor England.

SKARA BRAE, ORKNEY

On the west coast of Mainland – the main island of the Orkney archipelago off the north coast of Scotland – is a place called Skara Brae. It was once home to a Neolithic settlement that tells us a lot about how people dealt with poo in colder climates. The remains of the village, which were discovered in 1850, form a cluster of eight dwellings that people lived in between 3200 and 2500 BCE. **That means they were inhabited before the Egyptians built the pyramids!** What made them so special was that these dwellings had indoor toilets. **Phew!** No more going out into the freezing wind to bare their bums. **Thank goodness for that!**

The houses at Skara Brae were built into an old rubbish dump called a midden. It might sound a bit odd to have your house next to a dump, but actually it would have been perfect for insulating them against the cold. Covered, curved passageways linked the buildings, protecting as many people as possible from the harsh wet and windy weather outside. Drains came out from the huts, leading to streams that flushed away waste. It would've worked a charm, until of course things got REALLY cold and the streams – and poo – were frozen over. **No one wants to have to deal with ice-cold poopsicles!** Archaeologists also

...d jewellery, pottery and even gaming dice at the site. Who knows, maybe they played games on the loo!

You can go and visit the Orkney islands and see what is left at Skara Brae – but you'll be glad to know that their toilets are a bit more modern these days.

KNOSSOS, GREECE

The magnificent palace of Knossos on the Greek island of Crete was constructed by the Minoan civilisation over hundreds of years, the earliest part of it beginning around 3,900 years ago. It's known for its fabulous toilets and its link to the legendary labyrinth housing the mythological Minotaur!

> WHY DID THE MINOTAUR LIKE GOING TO HIS TOILET?
>
> BECAUSE IT WAS a-MAZE-ing.

Although we don't know much about the Minoans, we do know that they took their toilets seriously. They used large ceramic pans which could be flushed with water to empty poo and wee into stone sewers. And boy, did they need to get rid of their poo, because it's estimated that by 1700 BCE, a whopping 100,000 people lived in the palace complex and surrounding city!

And, if you believe the myth, you'll know that there was one **VERY SPECIAL** inhabitant of the palace – the **LEGENDARY MINOTAUR!** This epic monster, which was said to have the head of a bull and the body of a man, was believed to stalk the labyrinth below the vast palace complex. Many an Athenian youth lost their lives to the beast, until brave hero Theseus ventured inside the labyrinth to put an end to its wicked ways. He had help in his endeavour from Princess Ariadne, who provided him with thread that he used to find his way back once he'd slain the beast.

Poor, misunderstood Minotaur. Perhaps he was so grumpy and mean because of all the poo getting chucked in his direction from above!

Or, maybe he was fed up with wiping his bum with stones. **That's right, ancient Greeks used stones** called **pessoi,** or even used broken fragments of ceramic pots called **ostraka**. **That sounds scratchy and ouchy!** We know they did this because they wrote about it. There are also paintings showing people wiping their bums with stones. **What a strange art project!**

XI'AN, CHINA

The Terracotta Army are life-size clay figures that were found in the tomb of Qin Shi Huang, the first emperor of China. There are **over 8,000 of them**, all buried with the emperor in 210 BCE. Each sculpture is different, representing generals, cavalry, bowmen and many other different types of armed fighters. They were buried with the emperor to protect him in the afterlife. (He must have been expecting something scary waiting for him if he had that many people looking after him!)

In 2023, nearly 50 years after the army was discovered, archaeologists in Xi'an, China dug up something almost as impressive nearby – **the world's oldest flushing toilet!** It was the first ancient flush toilet of its kind ever discovered in China and in fact, it was the only one ever found! When the archaeologists realised they had dug up an ancient toilet, they all burst into laughter. Even serious scientists find toilets funny.

It was most likely that the toilet was used by officials of high rank during the early years of China's first unified empire. **Perhaps even the emperor himself!** Before he came to power, China was ruled by six separate, rival states. Shi Huang managed to bring them all together using a combination of warfare and bribery. He hoped his achievement would last ten thousand generations! (Not a modest man, then!) But sadly it only endured a few years after his death.

The fancy flushing toilet was made up of a box with a bent pipe coming out the bottom that would have led to a pit, where all the poo was sent. It would have needed someone with a big bucket to pour water into the top of it, to wash the poo away. It probably won't surprise you that it might have been servants who did that job rather than the high-status owners of the flushing toilet. They wouldn't do it themselves after the hard work of doing a poo.

AZTECS AND THEIR POOP CANOES

Deep in the heart of modern-day Mexico, there once stood a magnificent city. It was called Tenochtitlan, and it was the seat of the mighty Aztec Empire. It was constructed in 1325 CE on an island in the middle of Lake Texcoco, and at its height, a staggering 400,000 people lived there. Tenochtitlan was huge; bridges spanned waterways connecting different districts, and the streets were wide enough for ten horses to be ridden through. There were stunning floating gardens and beautiful ornate buildings.

But the city wasn't just good-looking; it also had lots of ingenious ways of keeping its inhabitants fed and its streets free from the diseases that poo can bring.

Clean water was brought to the city via aqueducts and waste was taken away on boats. Canoes were carefully placed underneath public toilets on the bridges and anyone needing to poo could sit on the edge, look out over the water and listen as their poop fell into the poop canoes below. **(I just hope they aimed well and no one was going for a swim underneath!)** When the poop canoes were full of human dung they would be towed away, and the fresh fertiliser would be spread on the floating gardens.

Poo is full of nitrogen and phosphorus, minerals that are great for helping plants grow.

If people didn't fancy venturing out, or it was night time, they would simply use buckets in their own homes.

Sounds gross, but it was fair enough really, because it was said that at night, a terrifying **ghost spirit** later named La Llorona, in the language of the Spanish who conquered the Aztec Empire, stalked the waters of the city. If you caught a glimpse of her, **something terrible would happen** and you might even die!

Definitely not worth that just to have a poo!

QUICK QUESTION

Now you've seen how ancient peoples across the world liked to do their poos, what about you? Which one of the weird and wonderful methods from the past would you prefer?

Ceramic pot like in ancient Mesopotamia?

Floating canoes like in Tenochtitlan?

A limestone throne like Queen Cleopatra herself?

CHAPTER THREE: THE VIKING AND THE GIANT POO

Have you ever wondered who did the world's biggest poo? No? **Well, it's a good job I have!** We can't say for certain that it's the world's biggest – after all, there isn't a poo inspector going round measuring them all, is there? No one would want to do that job! But one giant poo, laid down over 1,000 years ago by a Viking in York, certainly has a good claim to be the number one number two ...

WHO WERE THE VIKINGS?

Vikings were explorers, raiders, invaders, pirates and settlers who liked nothing more than sailing round the orthern and Western Europe, frightening the out of everyone they came across. They came from modern-day **Norway, Denmark and Sweden in their magnificent longboats**, looking for land and loot, and were at the height of their powers from the ninth to eleventh centuries. They were frightening foes who wore **heavy chainmail** and carried **fearsome axes and swords** – and they even worshipped **frightening gods**, too. There was the mighty Thor, a god of incredible strength, who went round swinging his hammer and using it to defeat giants. And there was Freyja, the goddess of death and war, who decided who would live and die in battle. **What a friendly bunch — why couldn't they have gods of friendship, happiness and peace, eh?**

When the Vikings weren't too busy raiding, they were also very good at trading, bringing with them goods such as silks, silver, jewellery and pottery wherever they went – **so, on balance, it wasn't all bad!**

47

QUICK QUESTION

There were many other gods and goddesses worshipped by the Vikings, with all sorts of epic powers. Which one would you like to have?

The 'trickster' god, Loki, was able to shape-shift into whatever he wanted – animal, human, you name it!

The god of light, Balder, was immune to any danger in the world (oh, except for one thing: mistletoe. Yep, that's right, he couldn't be killed by anything apart from a plant!).

Heimdall was a mysterious god who had the power to see things hundreds of miles away (I can do that with a telescope – no need to brag!).

VIKING BRITAIN

Nowhere was safe from the Vikings, and that included England, much of which had fallen into Danish hands by the end of the ninth century. One of those places was a town in northern England, which was invaded and settled by a Viking with a funny name, Ivar the Boneless, and his brother, Halfdan. They named it Jorvik, and today, it is known as York.

> **WHAT DO YOU CALL A VIKING KING'S FART?**
>
> **A NOBLE GAS.**

It was here, hundreds of years later in 1972, that archaeologists discovered something they weren't expecting – the fossilised remains of a ginormous poo! A Thor-level poo, if you will. A true hammer of the Norse gods. It was discovered along with wood, cloth and leather that was left behind from the settlement and it was studied in minute detail by its discoverer, an archaeologist called Dr Andrew 'Bone' Jones.

This **1,000-YEAR-OLD POO** measured a **GIGANTIC 20 cm long and 5 cm wide** and is believed to be the **BIGGEST** example of a fossilised human poo ever found.

'This is the most exciting piece of excrement I've ever seen,' wrote Dr Jones. 'In its own way it's as irreplaceable as the Crown Jewels!'

I thought *I* was excited about poo – this guy is on another level!

FOSSIL FAECES

But how did a mere poo survive all those years? Well, it was fossilised, that's how. A fossil is the remains of something old that has been embedded in rock or has turned to stone, and it's a process that takes place over many years. **Mineralisation is a type of fossilisation** – that's when organic items, such as plants or animal remains or even poop, are gradually replaced by different minerals, making them super hard. This is what happened to the giant Viking poo, which is why it kept its shape and size. It's funny to think that 1,000 years after our Viking left their GIANT poo, another human came along and picked it up, and now we can all go and see it. Just think about that the next time you poo – **it might live long into the future!**

DID YOU KNOW?

The proper name for a fossilised poo is a coprolite? If not, well, you do now!

Remember those Aztecs and their poop canoes, and how their poo made for great fertiliser that helped plants grow? Well, **fossilised poos are really good fertilisers** too, because of all the minerals locked up inside them. In the town of Ipswich in England there is even a road called Coprolite Street because there was once a factory there where coprolites were mined, crushed and turned into fertilisers.

Our Viking coprolite – which is named the Lloyds Bank coprolite because that was what was being built there when they discovered it – **was a very special find**. Mostly we only find big pits full of old poo mixed together, where people used latrines and pit systems to hold waste. But in this instance, we got this beauty all on its own – **lucky us!**

This poo is also special because it shows us exactly what this one person was eating at the time. For this, we need the help of people whose job it is to study ancient poo. They're called **paleoscatologists**, but I prefer to call them: **POO DETECTIVES!** They can tell us a lot about the humans who made the poo, such as what they ate and what was living inside their guts!

POO DETECTIVES

Scientists who analysed the giant poo discovered that the Viking who laid it was mostly living off a diet of meat and grains. It was a little surprising because nearby they also found fossilised remains of vegetables, fruits and fish, too. **That means that someone was choosing NOT to eat their vegetables!**

NAUGHTY VIKING!

But the fact that this Viking was a big old meat-eater wasn't the only thing scientists discovered. When they took a closer look under the microscope, they found a large number of tiny, microscopic eggs, which came from a parasitic organism. Parasites are any organism that lives inside another one, and in this case, the eggs came from **WHIPWORMS** and **MAW-WORMS**. These are small, round worms that live in the guts of humans – the adults of which can grow to be 2 metres long YUCK!

Having parasites meant that our Viking probably would have suffered from nasty tummy pains, diarrhoea and occasional fevers. What's even more disgusting

PRRRRP!

> BuRRRRRRP!

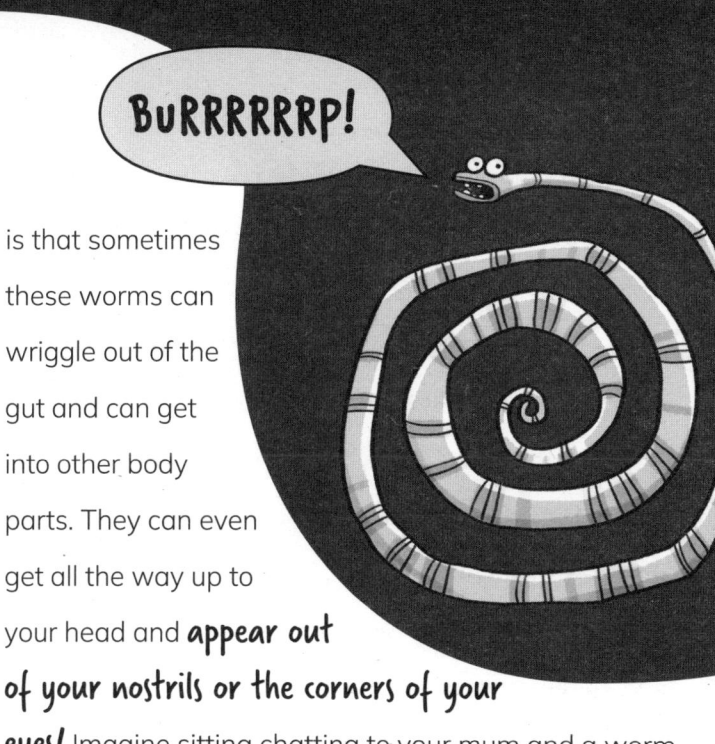

is that sometimes these worms can wriggle out of the gut and can get into other body parts. They can even get all the way up to your head and **appear out of your nostrils or the corners of your eyes!** Imagine sitting chatting to your mum and a worm appeared from her ear, crawling out to say hello to everyone. **Terrifying!**

A female whipworm wriggling about inside the guts can lay between **2,000 and 10,000 eggs per day**. Every one of those eggs could turn into a worm that would feed on the meat and bread that the Viking had been stuffing down, taking away important nutrients from their human host, as well as causing a lot of discomfort.

WASH IT ALL AWAY!

Worm infections come from water that has been contaminated by poo from other people who have the infection themselves, which is why it's so important to wash away poo and waste and keep it far away from fresh water supplies. Now we know that we can kill bugs in water by boiling it or by using water treatment tablets with chlorine in them, but the Vikings didn't know about all that. Where else could the Vikings have raided and traded if they hadn't been held back by wriggling tummy worms? They could have left their giant poops all over the world.

DID YOU KNOW?

The Vikings travelled far and wide. Their presence wasn't just felt in Britain.

- Coins with Arabic markings were found in Viking graves. They were picked up as far away as Baghdad in modern-day Iraq, by Viking traders.

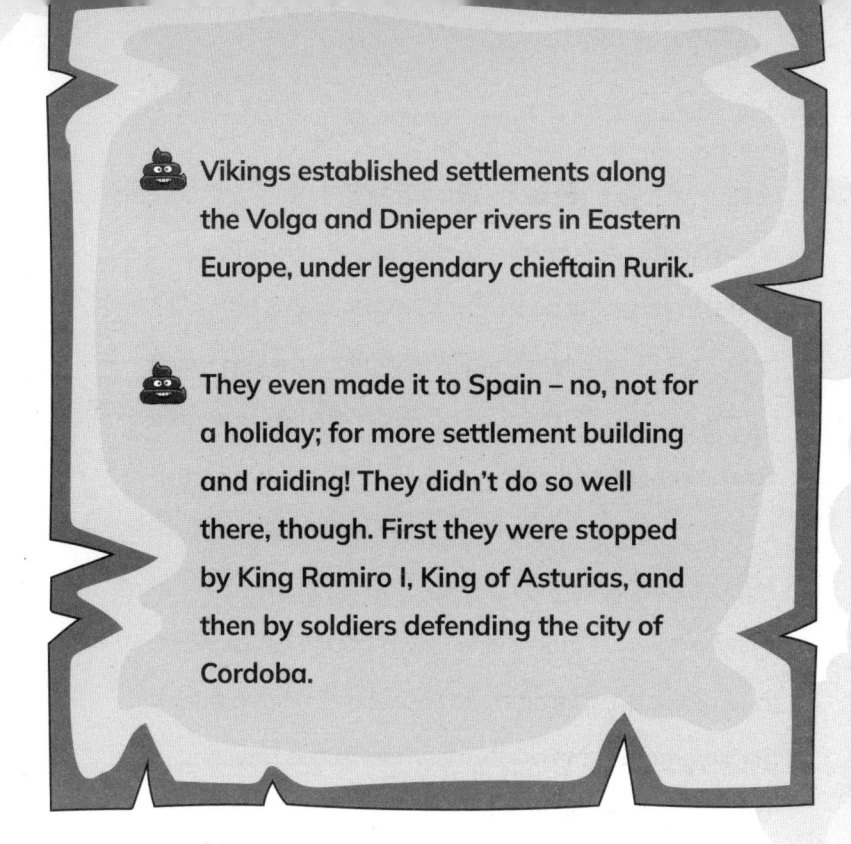

💩 Vikings established settlements along the Volga and Dnieper rivers in Eastern Europe, under legendary chieftain Rurik.

💩 They even made it to Spain – no, not for a holiday; for more settlement building and raiding! They didn't do so well there, though. First they were stopped by King Ramiro I, King of Asturias, and then by soldiers defending the city of Cordoba.

If you're feeling brave, you can go and see the old giant poo for yourself at the Jorvik Viking Centre in York, and **if you're really 'lucky' you might be able to smell how stinky it was**, because scientists have recreated the stench of it so that visitors can 'enjoy' the real experience. **Why, scientists, why?**

Sadly – or perhaps not – you won't be able to touch the poo. Once, when some children went on a school trip to see it, they dropped it on the floor and it broke it into three pieces. **Oh no!** It was repaired but it will never be one whole giant poo ever again. **Ah well, nothing good ever lasts!**

After hundreds of years of colonisation and settlement, the Viking age finally came to an end in Britain when the English King Harold Godwinson defeated the Norwegian King Harald Hardrada at the Battle of Stamford Bridge in 1066. That was followed shortly after by the Norman conquest of England, when Harold Godwinson was himself killed at the Battle of Hastings. **I wonder if that lot had better toilet habits?**

PROBABLY NOT!

CHAPTER FOUR: OLD MEDICINE for POOEY PROBLEMS

As hilarious as it is to encounter giant Viking plops or totally gross-out Roman bum brushes, the truth is, poo has caused us humans all sorts of problems through the ages. From stomach pains to trapped wind – or trapped toots if you prefer – our bowels and the poo that comes out of them have all sorts of issues. But whatever the pooey problems, there have been many **wonderfully weird** and **weirdly wonderful** ways us humans have treated them throughout history. **And lucky for you, you're going to read allll about them!**

ALL BUNGED UP

Constipation is the fancy word for when we get a bit bunged up and the poo just won't come out, no matter how hard we try. It can cause our tummies to swell up and it can be a really painful experience. Fortunately we have lots of ways to help the gut do its thing and make the poo come out, and over the centuries we have found different herbs and remedies that make our poo softer and easier to pass. **Ahhh, that's better!**

> HOW DID THE MATHEMATICIAN SOLVE HIS PROBLEM WITH CONSTIPATION?
>
> HE WORKED IT OUT WITH A PENCIL.

One of the oldest complete books that we know of is from the sixteenth century BCE. It is called the **Ebers Papyrus**, and it's one of the best-preserved records of medical knowledge from ancient Egypt. It contains descriptions of all sorts of different diseases and the most up-to-date understanding of anatomy and how the body worked. It suggests recipes and remedies and special incantations that are supposed to help with common ailments, **AND, most excitingly, it talks about poo!**

The Ebers Papyrus puts forward the idea that constipation is caused by poisoning of the body by waste decomposing inside the intestines. Now, this idea might sound possible, and it *was* believed for centuries, but it's actually **WRONG, WRONG, WRONG!**

In reality, what causes constipation is not drinking enough water and not having enough fruits, vegetables and fibre in your diet. **A bit like that giant-poo-laying Viking we met in the previous chapter!**

DID YOU KNOW?

Cleopatra, who was the last Egyptian pharaoh, would have known all about the Ebers Papyrus. We don't know if she was ever constipated, but we know she liked to experiment with all sorts of different remedies. She tried to:

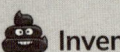

- 💩 Invent a cure for baldness

- 💩 Concoct her own painkillers

- 💩 Create powerful, ahem, poisons, to kill her enemies

Oh well, it's good to try different things, right?

Fast forwarding to the medieval period in Europe between the fifth and fifteenth centuries, people would use commonly available plants such as rhubarb, senna and liquorice root to help their tummies. **And how did they know how much to take? They just kept eating until they started to poo!**

BOWEL BLOAT

In Britain during the Georgian and Victorian times (from the seventeenth to nineteenth centuries), the makers of pills and potions would scare people into buying their medicines by calling constipation the dramatic-sounding *bowel bloat* and by saying it was caused by **'a horrible slimy monster that makes man's life a misery.' ARGH — RUN AWAY!** Adverts in newspapers would say: **'When the bowels stop working they become filled with putrid, rotting matter, causing poisonous gases that go through the whole body.'** Frankly, that's enough to scare ME into wanting some of their medicine and I *know* it's all rubbish!

The opposite of constipation is diarrhoea. **(Why do they make these words so hard to spell?)** Diarrhoea occurs when we poo too much, and instead of our poo being nice and solid, it gets sloppy and runny. Diarrhoea can be painful and upsetting and can be caused by anything from bacterial infections to viruses.

> Now, I can hear you asking: what makes a really good poo? And how do you know when you've got diarrhoea or constipation? Well, you've come to the right person! Doctors and scientists in the 1990s came up with the Bristol Stool Chart, which was designed to give you some idea of what a healthy poo looks like.

1. Little hard lumps are signs of constipation. Ouch!

2. A lumpy sausage shape is also a sign you're bunged up.

3. A sausage shape with cracks is normal. Hurray!

4. A snake-like poop is normal. Well done, you!

5. Soft blobs mean you could do with eating more fibre.

6. Mushy poop means you have mild diarrhoea.

7. Runny or liquid poo means SEVERE diarrhoea. Oh no!

Of course, there's lots of variation, so don't worry too much if your poos don't look exactly like these! Honestly – if you're feeling fine, there is really no reason to peer into the contents of your toilet bowl at all!

THE KING'S CONCOCTIONS

People who lived during the Tudor age in Britain (from the late fifteenth to the early seventeenth centuries) often used camomile, mint, ginger, honey or herbs to help relieve painful symptoms of constipation and diarrhoea. We actually still use them today to help with poorly tummies. **Thanks, Tudors!**

King Henry VIII – the monarch at the height of Tudor power – was himself very interested in medical matters, often making concoctions to help with any tummy problems he and his family members had.

He also wrote about how to keep everybody safe from diseases by moving out of the city and away to the countryside, if there was plague going round. (It's all right for some – not everyone can just dash to their house in the countryside!)

No amount of potions and lotions that he created could have helped Henry's poor wives, though. **The king was famous for having six of them – two of whom he beheaded!** (There'll be more on that later.)

MEDICINE CAN CAUSE SIDE EFFECTS

Some medicines that are important for treating other illnesses can also cause tummy problems. When a medicine is good at fixing one problem but causes another, that's called a **side effect**. Some medicines such as painkillers can stop the gut from moving and prevent poo getting out. It's always about finding a balance that makes us feel better. Sometimes people who have to take painkillers, like after an operation, have to take laxatives **(medicines that help us poo)** too because of the constipating side effects.

Some medicines such as antibiotics can be great for killing off bacteria that cause infections. They can save lives when people get really sick, but they can cause diarrhoea too. That's because there are millions of good bacteria that live inside our guts, happily living along with us and not causing any problems, until we attack them with antibiotics.

So, us humans have been attempting to look after our poo health for thousands of years. But the important thing to remember is to **eat your greens** and **drink plenty of water** to keep yourself nice and hydrated!

CHAPTER FIVE: MEDIEVAL MUCK

The medieval era began in the fifth century, with the fall of the Western Roman Empire, and lasted 900 years, until the birth of the Renaissance period in the fourteenth century. It's sometimes called the **Middle Ages** because it is sandwiched between the very, very, very old days, when ancient Romans, Greeks and Egyptians were doing their thing, and the modern era, which covers the fifteenth century up until our own time. The medieval period was a time of big change in society and politics, huge castles, noble and not-so-noble knights – but none of that changed the fact that humans needed to poo, **and boy did it STINK!**

THE ERFURT LATRINE DISASTER

The year was 1184 and a large group of nobles were gathering in a place called Erfurt in Germany. They came from across the lands of the **Holy Roman Empire** – a vast kingdom that stretched across Western and Central Europe. They were told to gather there by their king, Henry VI, who had just about had enough of their fighting. The nobles were always squabbling over land, and it was time to put a stop to it!

They met in the Petersberg Citadel, which was in the centre of the city. In keeping with many buildings of its size at the time, the church was built over a giant latrine. This wasn't like one of your fancy Roman sewer systems; it was simply a pit that was dug out to collect human waste deposited from above. **(Can you see where this is going?)** As the nobles piled into the big room, greeting old friends and meeting new ones, the floorboards began to creak. **Uh-oh.** The wooden floor broke apart under their weight and the floor gave way.

Down the nobles fell into the disgusting, stinking, plop-filled cesspit below.

GROSS!!

Sixty people died when they fell into the poo pit. Some of them were hit by falling rubble, some drowned under the poo and some even died because the noxious gases given off by the poo stopped them from breathing. Some tried to climb over others to get out, pushing them under the brown sludge.

King Henry was OK, though. He was sitting on something solid. Not a solid poo but a hard piece of stone that was now high up on the church wall (since the floor didn't exist any more!). Louis III Landgrave of Thuringia, one of the men causing the arguments, fell into the poo too, but he was able to scramble out and survive.

After all that, no one knows if they even resolved the land dispute they were there to talk about! I suppose the survivors had better things to think about, **like cleaning the poo out of their hair!**

POOP ON THE WALLS

In medieval villages and towns across Europe, folk would do their solid business into pails, or night buckets. They would then either take them to be emptied into communal pits or they would hand them over to **'gong farmers'**, who would go round collecting buckets of poo to be used as fertiliser in fields or gardens.

Powerful, wealthy landowners who lived in castles stayed inside to do their poos. **But that didn't mean their poos stayed inside with them! Oh no.** Some castles had little rooms built on to the side of them, called garderobes. Garderobes had wooden benches with holes in them for people to poo through; underneath was a chute that the poo would drop down. Some chutes were short and the poo would fall down the outside of the castle wall to the moat or courtyard below – **or sometimes stick to the walls!**

Others would have a longer shaft all the way down to the ground. Naturally, any mess would have to be cleaned up by servants. PFFT! TYPICAL!

> WHY DOES THE SUN NEVER SHINE ON CASTLES?
>
> THEY'RE FULL OF KNIGHTS!

MEDIEVAL CASTLES

In the Middle Ages, hundreds of castles were built throughout Britain and Europe. They were great for showing off the wealth and strength of the rich lords and ladies who lived there, and the high walls made of stone were perfect to hide behind if anyone tried to attack.

DID YOU KNOW?

Castles had lots of special features, including:

💩 Dungeons where you could chuck your enemies if they were getting on your nerves

💩 A 'keep', which is a big central tower which served as the last line of defence

💩 A great hall where all the fancy, important people had banquets and chilled out

💩 Wide, water-filled ditches called 'moats' around the outside. They were used for protection against enemies (who didn't like getting wet, apparently), and also as a place to flush your waste. Nice!

Sadly, not all castles had garderobes – some just had rooms covered with dried grass where people would do their poos. They tried to cover the area with herbs to mask the smell, but let's face it, herbs do nothing in the face of a stinky number two!

MEDIEVAL BUM WIPING

People didn't have nice clean rolls of toilet paper hanging in their garderobes like we do, and they didn't share a sponge on a stick as the Romans did. They also didn't use a rough stone like the ancient Greeks.

So what did they use? Drumroll please . . . they used **GRASSES or HAY or MOSS!**

(Aw, I was hoping it was going to be something fun, like turnips.)

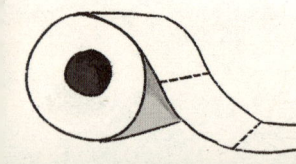

One monk in Bury St Edmunds wrote in the twelfth century that they nearly had a fire when a candle burned a little too close to the straw pile in the Abbey's privy. With noxious flammable gases and piles of straw, it's surprising we don't have more stories about fires starting in loos!

THE SOLDIERS WHO CLIMBED UP THE SLIMY TOILET CHUTE

Chateau Gaillard is a medieval castle in Normandy, France, built by the English king Richard the Lionheart in the 1100s. It was designed to protect his lands there, and it did so successfully until 1203, when French King Philip II decided he'd really rather like Normandy back. By that time, the chateau was owned by a weak ruler, King John, so Philip knew it was time to strike!

Unfortunately for Philip, the castle had three massive walls and a **stinky moat full of medieval poo bobbing about** to keep attackers out. **(Really, can someone invent a proper toilet already?)** Nevertheless, he lay siege to the castle, hoping that eventually the people inside would give up the defence.

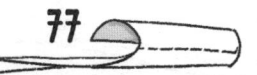

Some of Philip's men tried to mine underneath the walls but that was a tough job. Some tried to climb up the walls with ladders, but they didn't get far because the ladders were too short. **(Really, did someone not think to measure them?)** There was one other way into the castle, though: the toilet chute!

The toilet had been built on to the castle so that people didn't have to go far from church services if they had a call of nature. It was a convenience at first, but it soon became a chink in the castle's defences. **Philip's men climbed their way up the slippery, poo-spattered walls of the chute**, through the garderobe and into the castle's chapel. Once inside, they fought their way down to the front entrance and let their fellow soldiers in through the front gate. **The siege was over — Philip had WON.** King John wasn't even there though. He had left the area way back. Perhaps he was on the 'john' somewhere else, being quite comfy as king in one of his other castles over in England. **Such hardship!**

DID YOU KNOW?

Sieges were BIG in the Middle Ages; it was one of the main ways of waging war. Everyone wanted to capture castles, but it wasn't as easy as just wandering through the front door. When it came to sieges, there were some weapons that could help:

- 💩 Battering rams: giant logs mounted on wheels that soldiers could use to smash open a castle's heavy doors. OOF!

- 💩 Catapults: wooden contraptions that could shoot rocks, stones and flaming missiles. Sometimes they even catapulted dead, rotting animals over the walls to try and spread disease. (That's not very friendly is it?)

- 💩 Trebuchets: even bigger contraptions for when a catapult just won't do and you need to fire a rotting animal even further!

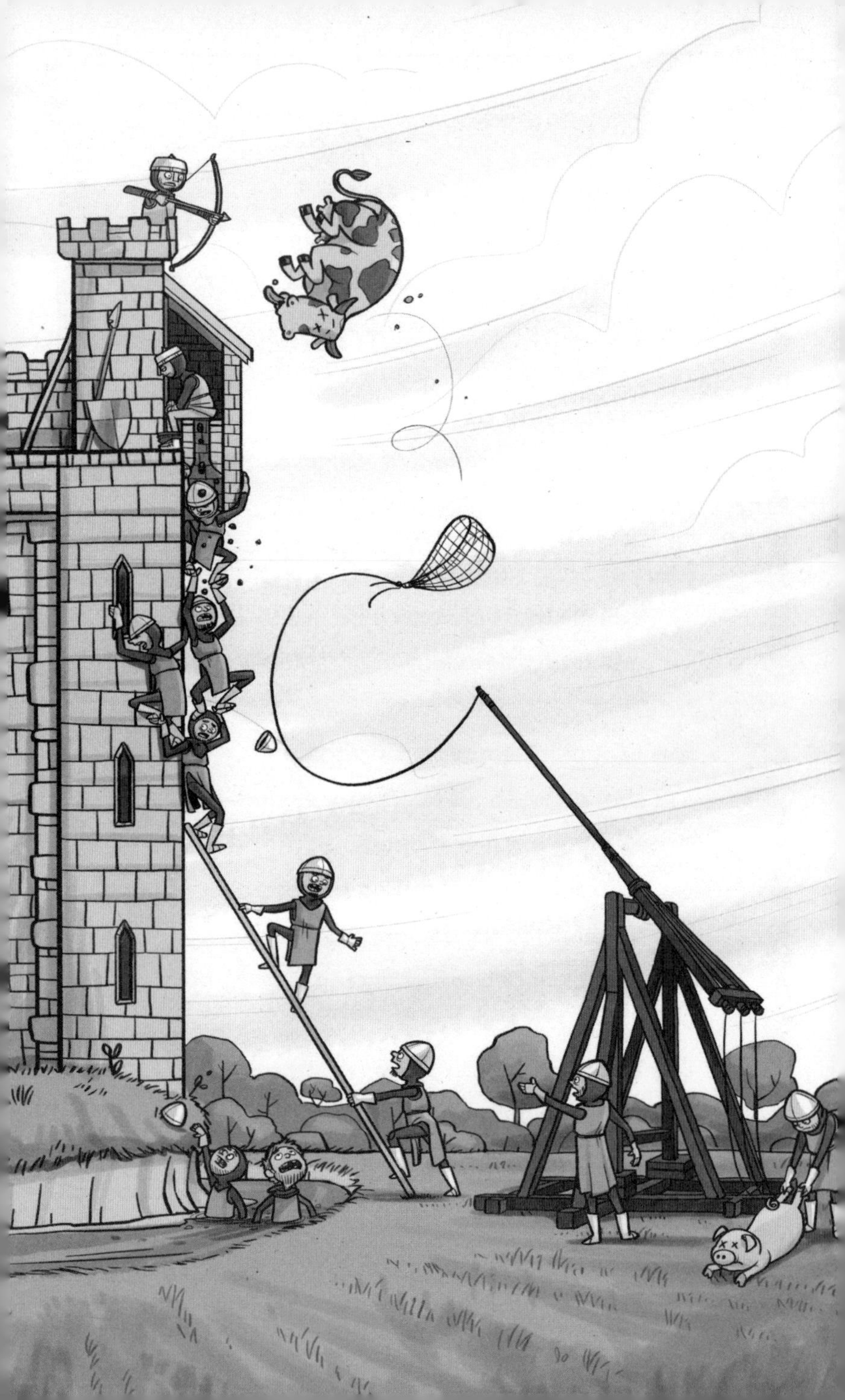

Apart from being really gross and horribly smelly, Philip's soldiers risked being overwhelmed by the gases being given off by the poo. They also risked sickness from the poo that they had to climb through – though they probably weren't really thinking about that at the time.

There were lots of changes that came after Chateau Guillard was attacked, and not just to the design of castle toilets. It upset the nobles in England that King John was losing land and castles to the French like that, and they rebelled against him. **Unlucky, John!**

POORLY TUMMIES IN THE MIDDLE AGES

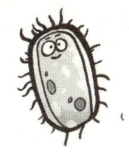

With all this talk of poo tumbling down castle walls and cesspits below churches, it is no wonder that people got sick. There are all sorts of diseases caused by different bacteria that can live in the gut – from *Salmonella* and *Shigella* to *Escherichia coli* (E. coli). **When anyone with the bugs inside them poops,**

the bacteria come out too. If people come into contact with them, they can easily become unwell. The body works hard to try and get rid of tummy bugs, which can cause diarrhoea, make your temperature go up and make you vomit. This is called dysentery and lots of people have died from it over the years.

In places where hygiene is difficult, like in medieval villages, castles or in soldiers' camps, dysentery can spread fast and cause a lot of problems. In 1307 **King Edward I, nicknamed Longshanks because he was really tall**, was on his way north to Scotland to have a fight with Robert the Bruce, the Scottish king. He didn't make it out of England before he started to feel unwell. He had pains and cramping in his stomach, felt sick and dizzy, and had fever and diarrhoea. **It got so bad that he died!** The soldiers left behind didn't want to fight any more and went home. **Until the next time.**

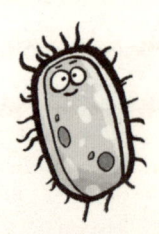

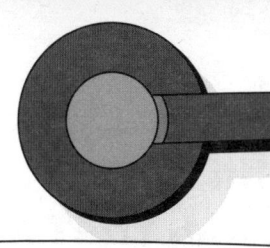

QUICK QUESTION

Longshanks is a magnificent name for a king. But what would you be called?

Queen Bigfoot? King Wobbly-Arm? Princess Knobbly-Knee?

Even better, what would you call your sibling? Prince Snotty-Bot? Princess Toenail?

In 1376, Longshanks' great grandson, Edward the Black Prince, a great knight of his age, may have died of dysentery too and so did King Henry V of England in 1422. **Dysentery doesn't mind if you're a great king or a humble peasant** – that's why we should all wash our hands after going to the loo!

HOW DID KNIGHTS POOP WHEN WEARING ALL THAT ARMOUR?

Medieval knights were known for their chivalry – which means being honest, kind and polite – and for their shining armour. **(Although, is it polite to carry around a big sword? Probably not!)**

Their armour was made of metal plates that deflected arrows and swords during a battle. But I know what you really want to ask . . .

HOW DID KNIGHTS IN SHINING ARMOUR DO A POO?

It wasn't the easiest thing to do, but it wasn't too difficult either. The flaps of armour that came down over the hips and bum were hinged and could be lifted. The knight would then squat over a hole in the ground or a bucket. When they stood up they could just drop the hinged plates back down again and walk away. **Easy!**

KING EDMUND IRONSIDE SHOULD HAVE LOOKED IN THE LOO!

The death of Edmund Ironside, King Edmund II of England, was pretty grim even by medieval standards, and it was probably quite smelly too. On 30 November in the year 1016, Edmund had a call of nature, so off he went to the toilet, lifted up his kingly robes, sat down, got out his phone to check the football results – probably – and then something awful happened . . . An assassin, hiding in the pit below the latrine, thrust his dagger up into the king's behind, killing him. **Ouch!**

Edmund Ironside was not the only person killed in this way. Two noblemen in the Czech kingdom of Bohemia – Jaromír, Duke of Bohemia, and Wenceslaus III – were also killed by daggers up their behinds when they sat down on the loo.

I don't know about you, but next time I go, **I'm going to double-check there's no one lurking in the bowl.** Also, I think it's time to move on from medieval muck – **it's all getting a bit treacherous!**

Chapter Six: Tudor Number Twos

The Tudors were a noble family who came to rule England in 1485, when Henry Tudor beat King Richard III at the Battle of Bosworth. The battle marked the end of the War of the Roses between the houses of Lancaster and York, and the beginning of the modern period in British history. However, anyone going to the toilet in Tudor times might be forgiven for thinking **it wasn't all THAT modern!** People in the Tudor period were still using chamber pots, holes in the ground and garderobes. **And what's worse, the Tudors had a serious sewage problem . . .**

TUDOR TOWNS

In Tudor towns, open drains often ran down the middle of the streets, leaving it to rainwater to wash away what was thrown in there. **Can you guess what ended up floating down the middle of the road? THAT'S RIGHT — POO!** Chamber pots – big round bowls that were kept under the bed in case you needed to use the toilet at night – would be simply chucked out the window and into the street, right into the stream of filth running down the road.

> **WHAT'S THE BEST TIME TO GO TO THE TOILET?**
>
> **POO-THIRTY.**

Friendly Tudors who at least had SOME manners would shout out 'gardyloo!' to warn any passers-by that a pile of poop was about to come flying through the air. (Gardyloo comes from the French ***gardez l'eau***, and means 'watch out for the water'.)

Just be thankful next time you walk down the street that you're not going to be hit in the face with a nasty surprise. **YUCK!**

FOOD FIT FOR A KING

King Henry VII, the one that biffed Richard III at Bosworth, established his rule and settled things down in England. Under his kingship, the country became wealthier, which meant that some people, particularly nobles, had more money to spend on food. One man who loved his food was Henry VII's son, imaginatively named . . . wait for it . . . Henry VIII!

DID YOU KNOW?

Henry VIII was famous for many things: his appetite, the founding of the Church of England, but most famously of all, his six wives, who met a variety of different ends. You can remember who's who by learning the rhyme shown in the bold words.

DIVORCED – Catherine of Aragon

BEHEADED – Anne Boleyn

DIED – Jane Seymour

DIVORCED – Anne of Cleves

BEHEADED – Catherine Howard

SURVIVED – Catherine Parr

Henry VIII and his courtiers had a diet that was very fancy compared to his poorer subjects. He ate lamb, beef and chicken baked into elaborate pies, as well as deer and wild boar that he hunted on his estates. **Occasionally he ate pigeons and swans too! No animal was safe!** The king would also have sugar and exotic spices shipped from faraway countries, which were hard to get unless you had lots of money.

The poorer people of Tudor times had a very different diet from their rulers. They ate preserved rather than fresh meat and fish, and lots of vegetables. Spices such as cinnamon, cloves, garlic and vinegar would be used to disguise any meat that had started to go off. Adults, and even children, often drank weak alcoholic drinks such as beer, cider or mead **(which is made from honey)** because it was a lot safer than water. (I mean, come on, Tudors – there's poo running down the middle of the street, **of course the water wasn't safe!**) Our water is clean now, and definitely safer for kids than anything with alcohol in it!

GROOM OF THE STOOL

It wasn't just what went *in* to Henry VIII that was so important, though, it was also what came out. Believe it or not, the king had a special servant whose job it was to look after his bum, his toilet and anything that he left in his chamber pot, to make sure the king was in good health.

He was known as the **'Groom of the Stool'** – and it was a **VERY IMPORTANT** position. Having a good sniff and a poke about in what the king left behind would give the Groom of the Stool a good idea of the king's health. If the poo was **runny, sloppy or smelly, the king might have a tummy infection**. If his poo was **really hard or small, then the king might be bunged up**. If doctors thought the king's poo suggested he was unwell, they might give him an enema **(a medicine that goes directly up the bum to make the king poop more)** or they might make him swallow a medicine that would deliberately make him sick.

Being Groom of the Stool was a stinky task, especially the bit where he had to **wipe the King's bum!** It certainly wasn't a job for any man picked from the streets of London. After all, for anyone to get *that* close to the king, they would have to be someone he could trust. (Just ask poor Edmund Ironside about people getting too close to him in the toilet.)

QUICK QUESTION

What would you call your own personal groom of the stool?

The poo inspector?

The personal plop-person?

The dung detective?

Perhaps you can come up with your own name!

Henry VIII's daughters, Queen Mary I and Queen Elizabeth I, didn't have grooms of the stool, they had **ladies in waiting**. They weren't called that because they were *waiting* for their queen to poo; it meant that they were *waiting on* the queens. Though having said that, they *would* have to ensure that the queens' chamber pots were empty. **Lucky them!**

PERSONAL TOILETS

Henry VIII's 'close stool' was the height of **lavatory luxury** and would **travel with him wherever he would go** – which is a lot easier when you have someone else to carry it around for you! Imagine having to carry your own toilet to school and back!

The close stool was a **wooden box seat with a plush velvet cushion around the hole**. It allowed the king to sit comfortably rather than having to squat on the ground. It was **covered with sheepskins and decorated with ribbons**, and there was a space underneath for a pot. When the king lifted his robes and lowered his bare bum, it would be **nice and soft and not cold at all**. It also had a lid that could be shut to keep in any disgusting pongy smells.

> **KNOCK, KNOCK!**
>
> **WHO'S THERE?**
>
> **I NEED A PUH!**
>
> **I NEED A PUH-WHO?**
>
> **WELL, GO AND FIND SOMEWHERE TO DO IT THEN!**

It wasn't just in England where royals had luxury toilets and personal poo assistants. In France and elsewhere, kings and queens had close friends who would help wipe their bums and look after their poo, making notes on any unusual poops that might pass under their noses. The close stool used by Louis XIV, the extravagant **'Sun King'** of France, in the sixteenth century, was decorated with intricate carvings and soft, luxurious fabrics. The king's portable potty was not just a comfortable piece of furniture to poop on but was also **a symbol of his power and wealth**. It said to people: don't mess with the man who can afford such an elaborately decorated poop stool!

Henry VIII did build a toilet block for lower ranks of courtiers around him – **how kind!** It was known as the **Great House of Easement**. Fourteen people could be seated there at a time. It was a very different experience to using the personal, luxury cushioned seat that the king had. Although some loos like these were known as 'privies', coming from the old French for 'private', **they would have been anything but!**

HOW DID THE TUDORS WIPE THEIR BUMS?

Although there is evidence that the Chinese and Japanese had toilet paper over a thousand years ago, the Tudors living in England 500 years ago did not. Instead, much like their medieval ancestors, they used straw, leaves and mosses to wipe themselves clean.

A particular type of moss called **Sphagnum** soaks up water very well, so that would have helped clean things up too. If you're out for a walk and you see some moss, pick a bit up and give it a squeeze to see how much water comes out.

Monarchs and other wealthy Tudors might have also used **lamb's wool to wipe their bums, or bird feathers**, which would have been much softer. If you're out for a walk and you see a lamb, don't go picking at its wool – it won't like that very much.

WILLIAM SHAKESPEARE ON TUDOR TOILETS

William Shakespeare is probably the most famous English writer **EVER**, and he was busy writing his plays during Tudor times. He wrote about all sorts – kings, queens, doomed love, witches, magicians and . . . **BUMS, POOS and FARTS!**

In his play about King Henry IV, one minor character staying at an inn complained of having no access to a chamber pot, or a 'jordan', as they were also known. **(For any readers out there called Jordan, I can only apologise.** Apparently, they were named that after the water medieval pilgrims brought back from the Holy Land of Jordan. It's nothing to do with you, honest!) This character had to do his business into the fireplace. **I hope it wasn't lit!**

In Shakespeare's play *All's Well That Ends Well*, the character known as the Clown mentions the use of a close stool. He most likely wouldn't have had one himself as these belonged to the rich. He was most likely talking about the king's private potty – it would have been very brave of him to use that!

After all that toilet trouble, silky stools, open sewers running down the street and more King Henrys than you can shake a swan at, it's almost time to bring the chapter to a close. **BUT** – there is one final thing to look forward to. Towards the end of the reign of the Tudor dynasty, a godson of the queen FINALLY invented something we can all be very grateful for today: a proper, modern flushing toilet.

AT LAST!

What took them so long?

CHAPTER SEVEN: A ROYAL FLUSH AND DYING FOR THE LOO

It's the moment you've all been waiting for – finally, someone has invented the flushing toilet. **WOO HOO!** No more pooing in holes and squatting over latrines. **(Well, so long as you're wealthy enough to have one, of course.)** It was invented by a man called Sir John Harington in the 1590s. He was a courtier to Queen Elizabeth I – Henry VIII's daughter – as well as being a poet, writer and translator. **What a guy!** Sadly, as we'll see later on in the chapter, not everyone had the best of time on the loo – **but first, let's see how it works!**

101

THE AJAX

Sir John was Queen Elizabeth I's godson, as well as her courtier, which meant he got to spend a lot of time hanging around the royal palaces with her many advisors and companions. That was until he fell out with the queen and she **BANISHED HIM! But what was his crime?** Well, he translated an Italian poem into English to entertain the courtiers, but he made it **very, very rude**. Perhaps he loved a poo joke and Elizabeth wasn't keen. **Either way — he had to leave.**

Never mind – John went off to live in the countryside in his fancy country house, and it was there that he invented and installed the flushing toilet. **He called it the Ajax, after 'jakes', which was a slang word in Tudor times for a latrine.**

WHAT DID ONE TOILET SAY TO THE OTHER?
YOU LOOK FLUSHED!

The toilet was a two-foot-deep oval ceramic bowl, which was kept waterproofed with resin and wax. That meant waste would wash off it easily – **PHEW!** It had levers and pulleys to make it work, rather than a simple button like we have now. AND it needed a whopping 34 litres of water for a single flush, **which is over 100 drink cans' worth!**

Eventually, once the queen had forgiven Sir John for his rudeness, she came to visit him and he showed off his invention. **She loved it so much, at first, that she had one installed in one of her homes,** Richmond Palace. But, when it came to it, Elizabeth refused to use it because it was far too noisy and terrifying – **what a wimp!** She carried on using her close stool, which was nice and cushioned and cosy after all. (I bet the servant who had to clean up after her was really pleased about that.)

DID YOU KNOW?

Queen Elizabeth I was one of the most famous queens in English history, so we should probably learn a little bit more about her than where she went for a poo!

- 💩 Elizabeth was the daughter of Henry VIII and Anne Boleyn (one of the wives who got her head chopped off!).

- 💩 She was crowned queen in 1558 after the death of her sister, Mary, the first daughter of Henry VIII. She reigned for an incredible 44 years!

- 💩 When the Spanish King, Philip II, sent a fleet of ships, called the Armada, to invade England, Elizabeth gave a passionate speech to encourage her troops before they set sail to defend the country. Famously, the Spanish were defeated, and Elizabeth was a hero!

💩 She had red hair, just like her father, and wore thick white make-up to cover the scars left from an illness called smallpox.

💩 Elizabeth was the last Tudor monarch. She was succeeded by her cousin, James Stuart.

It took a long time for the flushing toilet to be accepted in England. One of the big problems was that it was all rather stinky. Smelly gases would build up in the pipes and they would come back up through the toilet to **pong out** anyone nearby.

What was needed was an ingenious little invention known as the **'S-bend'. S-bends are simply pipes that are shaped like the letter S**. After you flush, they get filled with a little bit of water, and this water stops any gases coming back up through the pipes.

Wahey! No more stink!

The first patent for a flushing toilet was not granted until 1775 to the Scottish inventor Alexander Cummings. That patent – a special licence from the authorities – meant that he had the exclusive right to sell his version of the toilet. Some years later, a Yorkshireman named Joseph Bramah added a hinged lid to his version of the toilet, which was great, because it meant that the water inside wouldn't freeze over **(or the poos!).**

THOMAS CRAPPER TAKES THE CREDIT

Lots of people think that a chap called Thomas Crapper invented the flushing toilet, because we sometimes call toilets crappers. **(Though that's quite a rude term now so I wouldn't use that if I were you!)**

But as we know, he **DIDN'T** invent them. What he **DID** invent were better ways of using them, including adding a ball cock to the cistern **(the box above the toilet),** which helps make sure the toilet is ready to flush when you need it.

Thomas Crapper sold lots of his toilets and they had **his name written on them, too,** so when people went to use one, they saw his name.

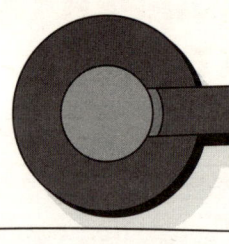

QUICK QUESTION

What big invention would you add to the toilet to make it better?

Flashing lights and speakers so you can have a toilet disco?

A special flush that gives you a lovely spray of perfume when you're done?

A built-in tablet so you can watch TV while you go?

That's how the mistaken idea that he was the inventor of toilets caught on. Over time, toilets began to be built into more and more homes, which was a lot more convenient AND warmer than traipsing outside.

It's a system that has been developed and tweaked over many years by lots of different people. Nowadays, even more technology is being added to improve toilets, especially in Japan. There, they have **heated seats and jets of water for cleaning your bum**. I wonder how Queen Elizabeth would have felt about that!

KING GEORGE II'S ROYAL WIND

As fantastic as loos are, not everyone has had a great time on them over the years. In fact, occasionally they've been downright deadly. Just ask George II, King of England. Now there was a man who kept a close eye on his watch. Everything he did was to a strict timetable, even his poos. Perhaps he learned his timekeeping skills when he was in the army – he was the last English king to appear on the battlefield.

One fateful day he woke at his usual time, had his usual cup of hot chocolate and went to the bathroom for his daily wash and to do his morning business.

It was then that his servant said he heard a noise coming from the bathroom that was very different to the usual **'royal wind.' (Imagine knowing what the usual royal wind sounds like?)** The servant opened the door to find the king on the floor with his trousers round his ankles. He was very sick, but not dead, until the servants dragged him back into his bed, where he promptly died. It turned out he had a problem with his heart that just couldn't take the pressure of going for his morning poo. **Poor guy!**

CATHERINE THE GREAT FELL TO THE BATHROOM FLOOR

Catherine the Great was Queen of Russia. After overthrowing her husband, Peter III, she reigned for over 30 years, from 1762 to 1796. Her rule saw **wonderful advances and changes in Russia** – the founding of new cities and a flourishing of the arts and sciences. **But even great queens have to poo.**

One day in 1796, whilst trying to do a royal number two, Catherine collapsed. The thing that made her so poorly was a stroke. Strokes happen when a blood clot (a clump of blood cells) lodges somewhere in the brain and stops blood from getting through to the brain tissue that needs it. They mostly occur in people over sixty-five.

When strokes happen, they can make it hard to move arms and legs and sometimes make it hard to speak or, worse, they can leave people unconscious.

Catherine's servants picked her up from the cold floor by the toilet and took her to bed, but she died the next day. It was a sad way to go. Sometimes people call the toilet a throne. **So, Catherine the Great almost died on the toilet throne whilst sitting on the royal throne!**

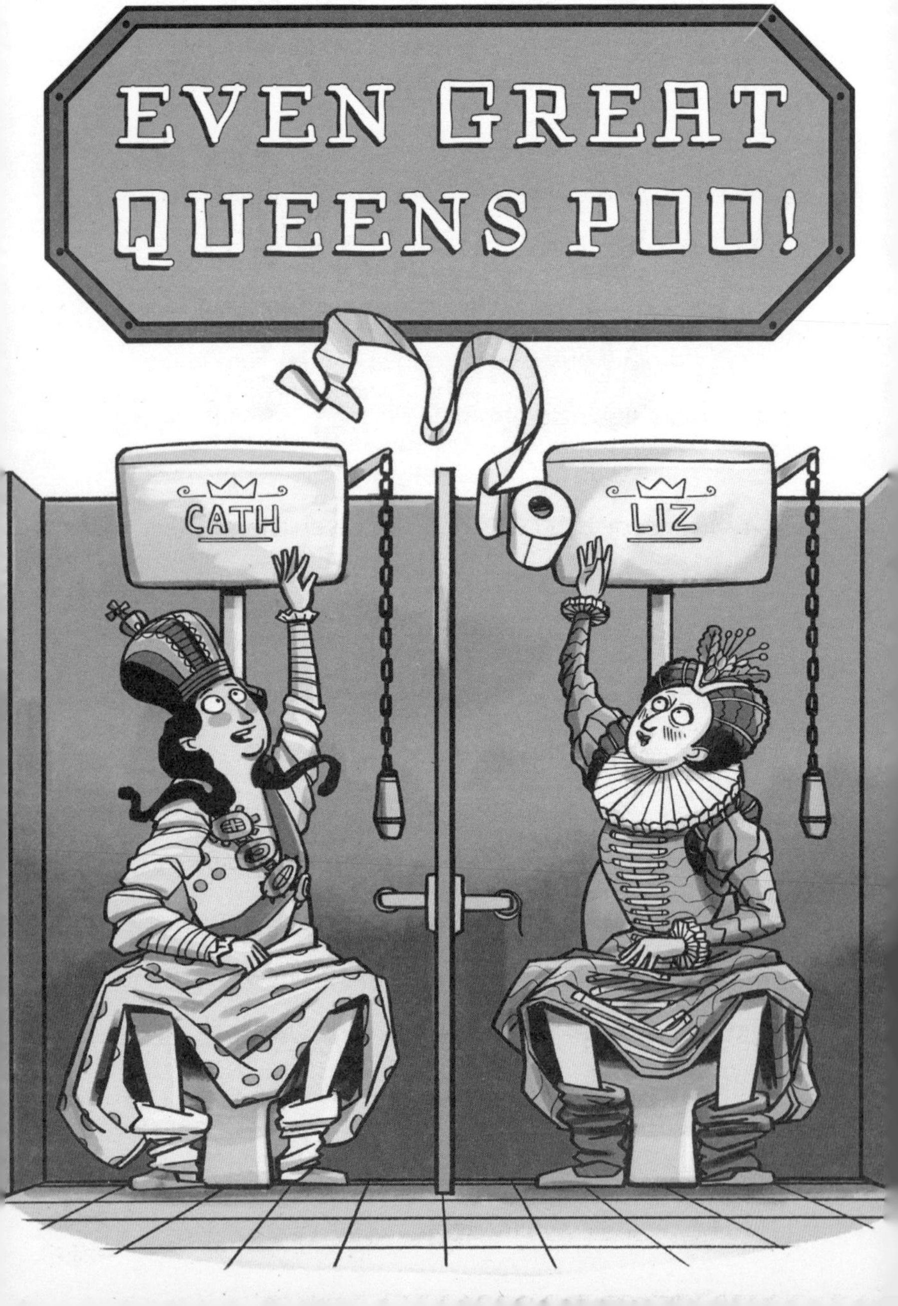
EVEN GREAT QUEENS POO!
CATH
LIZ

CHAPTER EIGHT: VICTORIAN WHIFFS

The summer of 1858 was hot. The River Thames that runs through London was drying up, and there was much less water flowing through it than normal. At the time, **London was the largest city on Earth**. In fact, it was the **largest city that history had ever known**. It had over 2 million inhabitants, many coming from all over the world to find their fortunes in the big city. But that many people produce a lot of poo, and soon it started to pile up on the dry and dusty riverbanks. **London was in for a seriously smelly summer . . .**

SERIOUS PONGS

By 1858, Queen Victoria had been on the throne of the United Kingdom for over 20 years. **(Not the toilet throne; she wasn't constipated, as far as we know. I mean the REAL one!)** Her reign was known for great advances in science, industry and trade, with the UK rising to be a superpower on the world stage.

One day, she and her husband, Prince Albert, tried to go for a nice pleasure boat cruise along the Thames, but they didn't get very far. The smell rising up from the riverbanks got so bad that they had to cancel their plans and turn back to shore. Even Victoria, with all that power and influence, couldn't stop the dreaded pong seeping up her royal nostrils. **URGH — how dare it?** No more pleasure boating for the queen and her prince! London, a great capital city of the world, was gross! **Victoria was very upset about it, and when Victoria was upset, something had to be done.**

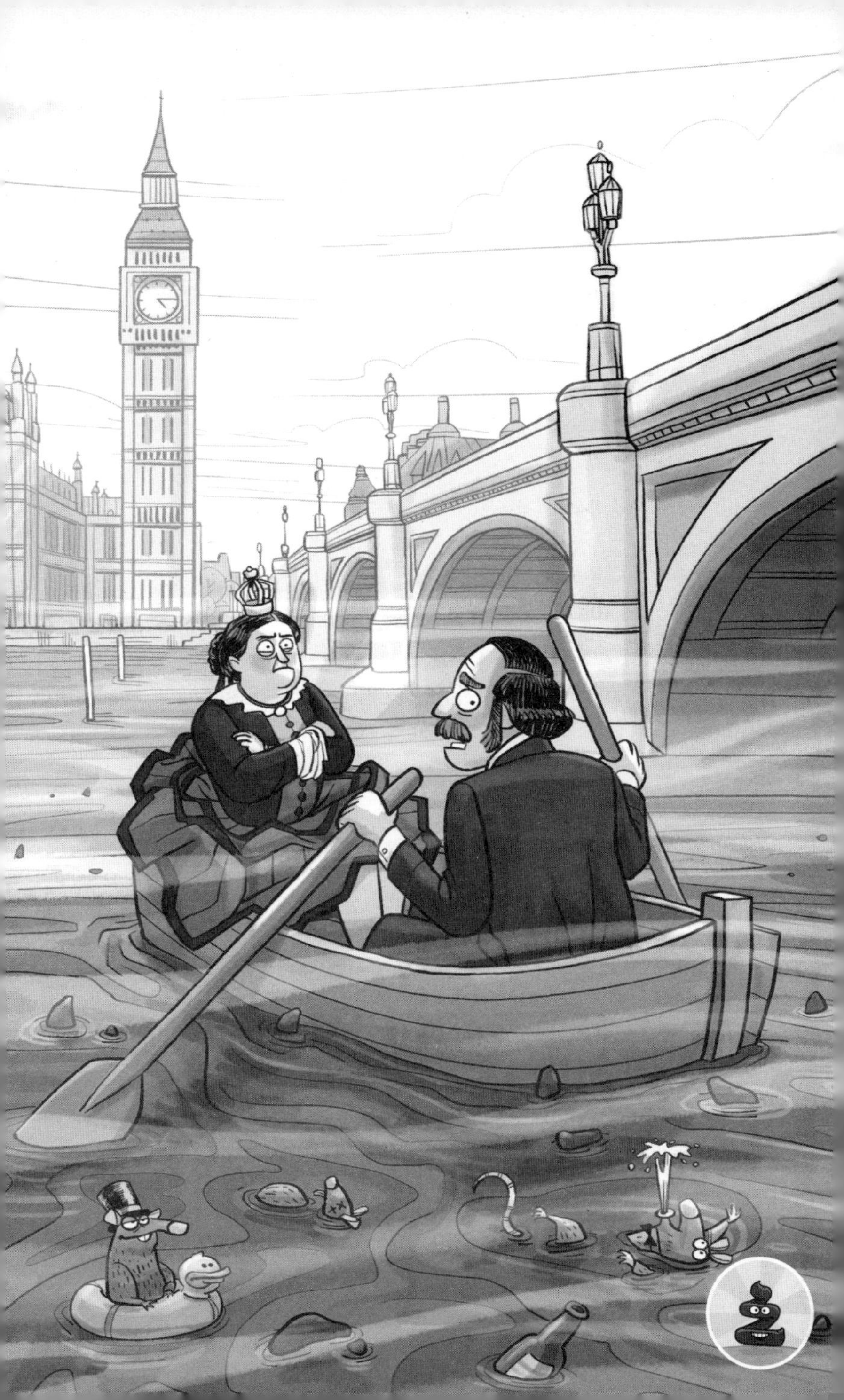

DID YOU KNOW?

Queen Victoria reigned for over 63 years, the second longest reign in British history. She had such an impact that the whole era was named after her. (Maybe one day they'll name the modern day after me! Or maybe you! Or maybe not.)

- Victoria's first name wasn't actually Victoria. Er, what? That's right – it was Alexandrina! Victoria was her middle name, and she just preferred it. Just think, instead of the Victorian era, we could have been talking about the Alexandrinian!

- She is sometimes known as the grandmother of Europe, because her children and grandchildren sat on thrones of many European countries, including Russia and Germany.

- Her most famous quote is 'We are not amused', but she might not even have said it! Aw, I like to imagine someone told her a poo joke and she wasn't having any of it!

It wasn't just Queen Victoria who was upset. The Houses of Parliament in London, which are right next to the river, were also affected by the smell. **It got so bad that the politicians couldn't do their work.** They even thought about evacuating the buildings and taking government business to Oxford.

By now the newspapers had given the whiff a name: the Great Stink. (Whether there'd be anyone left in London to read newspapers was another story!)

And even famous novelists, such as Charles Dickens, were mentioning it in their works. One of his characters, in a book called *Little Dorrit*, said that the Thames was **'a deadly sewer . . . in place of a fine fresh river'.** Now that's not very nice at all – **but it was probably true.**

People in charge tried to spread lime on to the riverbanks. **(I don't mean the lovely fresh citrus fruit – although maybe they should have tried that!)** Lime is a type of mineral that they hoped would mask the smell. But no, they were wrong – there was still a nasty pong (ooh, rhyming!). When that didn't work, they had to resort to more permanent measures.

LONDON'S SAVIOUR

The man to fix it all was called Joseph Bazalgette. Bazalgette was a civil engineer – **that's someone who designs and builds structures such as bridges, roadways, railways and sewers**. Bazalgette was chief engineer of the Metropolitan Board of Works; he was a clever, hard-working and determined man who came up with a **great solution to the Great Stink**. His plan was to make London's sewers bigger and better so that people could breathe again without getting a nose full of other people's poo gases.

There were already a lot of sewers under the city, which were built to move water about, but they were getting old and creaky. Some were left by the Romans, who had used clay pipes. Others were made of lead or **even hollowed-out trees!** There were also hundreds of cesspools underneath buildings that were draining out into the sewers, which they just couldn't handle any more. **AND** it was made worse by the new flushing toilets that added more filthy water into the mix **(where are those royal close stools when you need them?).**

Bazalgette designed sewers and pumping stations with big engines that **pumped away all the poop**. He planned for 132 kilometres of brick-lined underground tunnels and over 683 kilometres of street sewers to move the dirty water along. He was also clever enough to make **bigger sewers than were needed, so that they could cope if more people came to live in London** — which they did.

The pumping stations weren't just practical; they were actually so beautiful that they are now listed buildings, which means that they are protected from anyone wanting to change them. Though they weren't quite finished, Edward, Prince of Wales opened the sewers in 1865. **What a difference it made to the city!**

Sadly, the pumping stations pumped waste further down the river, **which wasn't always ideal**. When the Princess Alice pleasure boat that was sailing along the Thames hit disaster and capsized, it went down near one of the sewer outlets.

Many of the passengers were overcome with the fumes and gases coming from the stream of poo, and died!

DID YOU KNOW?

Bazalgette's sewers weren't the only engineering miracles in the Victorian age.

- Henrietta Vansittart was a self-trained engineer. She came from a very humble background but went on to design a ship's propeller that vastly increased speed and efficiency through water.

- Robert Stephenson designed the first bridge in the world to allow for rail and road traffic at the same time. It's called the High Level Bridge, and it crosses the River Tyne in Newcastle.

- Sarah Guppy was an inventor and was the first woman to patent a bridge as well as all sorts of useful products. She helped design Thomas Telford's Menai Bridge too. She died just before the Great Stink came along so she didn't have the misfortune of smelling it.

NIGHT-SOIL MEN

Before the sewers took the poo away, Londoners had to use cesspits. **But what happens when there's so much poo it no longer fits in the pit?**

Well, that's why you have to empty them, and that's where night-soil men came in.

Night-soil men were hired by homeowners to come to their houses in the middle of the night, when everyone was asleep, and take away the foul-smelling piles of poo that had built up in their cesspits during the day. They worked in teams of four, consisting of **a rope man, a hole man and two tub men**.

First, they would lift the floorboards or stones that covered the cesspit entrance and remove any overflowing poo. Then, the rope man would lower the hole man into the pit, and he would scoop out the rest.

I like to think of it as MISSION IM-POO-SIBLE!

The poop would be shovelled into tubs and passed up to the tub men, who would carry them away to their carts waiting outside. **So long as we've been leaving poo lying around, someone has had the job of moving it!**

> **WHICH KIND OF POO JOKES SHOULD YOU NEVER TELL?**
>
> **CORNY ONES!**

Night-soil men would take the carts sloshing about with poo to farmers outside the city walls, who would spread it on the fields as fertilisers. Later, someone came up with a technique to take a gas called nitrogen out of the poo and turn it into gunpowder for use in guns and cannons on battlefields. Suddenly poo became very valuable.

Being a night-soil man was a horrible, stinking job, and it was dangerous, too. The methane gases given off by the poo could explode if they came into contact with the flame from the night-soil men's lamps. That might singe the eyebrows or, far worse, burn houses down. They were well paid compared to other skilled workers, but honestly, thank goodness for proper sewers!

DID YOU KNOW?

💩 There were over 100 sewers built in London to deal with the Great Stink. PHEWWW!

💩 Before they built the sewers, there were 200,000 cesspits in London. That's a lot of work for the night-soil men!

💩 By the end of the nineteenth century, there were around 50,000 horses on the streets of London every day, producing around 20,000 tonnes of manure a month. That much manure posed a risk to health, what with all those nasty diseases spread through poo. Things became so bad it was known as the Great Manure Crisis – people thought they would soon be drowning in poop! But the poo-pocalypse never came to pass – with the invention of the car, horses weren't needed for transport any more. No more poo! (But more exhaust fumes . . . boooo!)

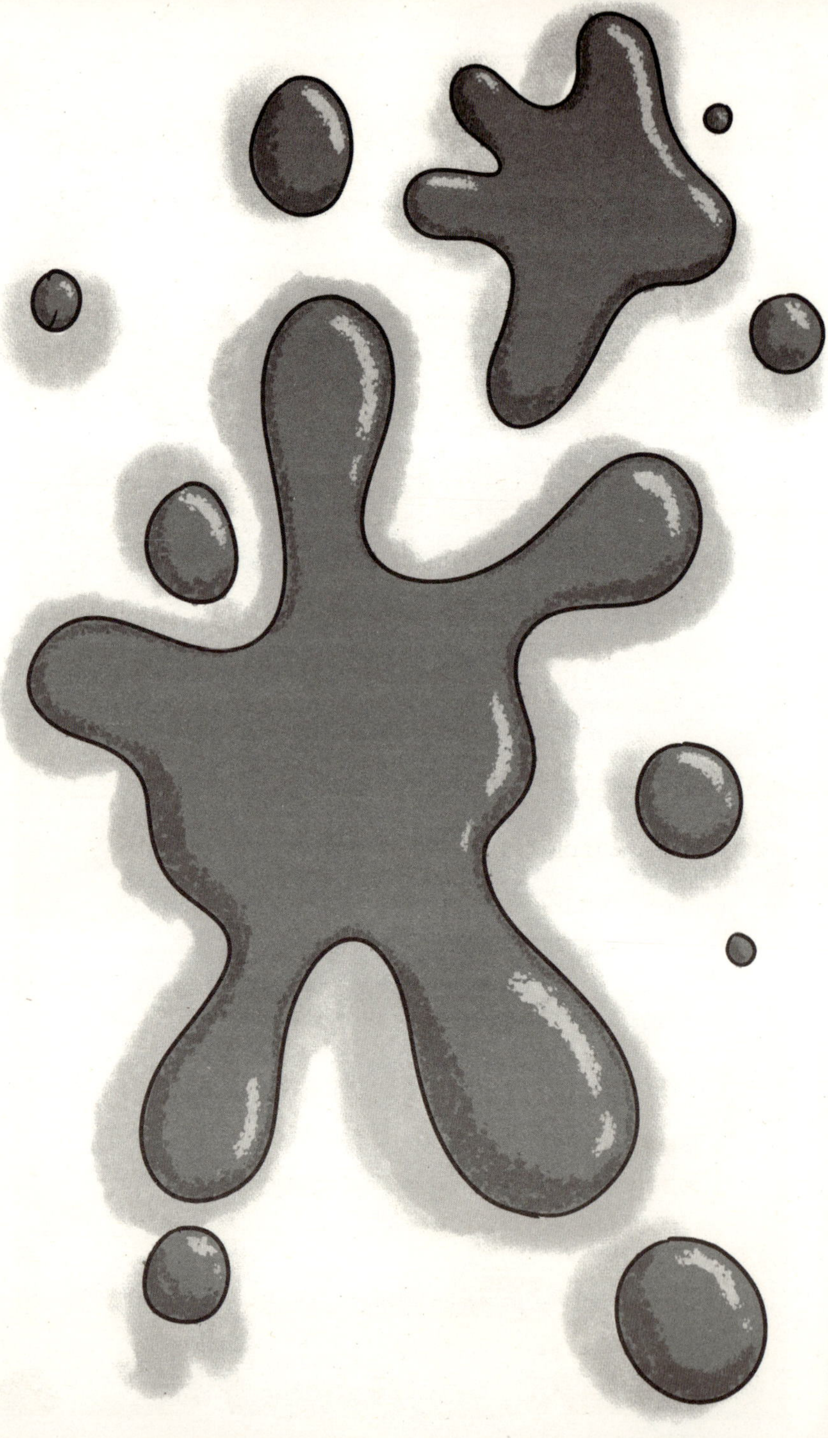

CHAPTER NINE: BEASTLY BACTERIA

Until about 150 years ago, people across the world believed that diseases were spread by nasty, smelly odours given off by rotting matter, such as dead animals and piles of poo. They called these odours **miasma**, but they were also known as 'bad air' or 'night air'. Apparently, just one whiff of this bad air scurrying up your nostrils would be enough to make you ill.

It sounds like it makes sense, right?

Well, it's all rubbish, actually. Sorry!

We now know that there are lots of different ways diseases are spread. Yes, some viruses like colds and flus are breathed in from the air, but it's not the air itself that's bad, **it's those pesky microbes!** There are viruses, parasites and even fungi that can sneak into our bodies when we're not paying attention, by getting into cuts and grazes on our skin or into our stomachs when we eat or drink them.

That's why we need to wash and keep clean. Bad bacteria can lurk everywhere, especially in food that's gone off. But do you know where you can also find lots of bacteria? **You guessed it — poo!**

> Before we learn about some of the nasty bacteria that make us sick, it'll probably help to understand what bacteria actually are, eh? Well, look no further than these top five facts!

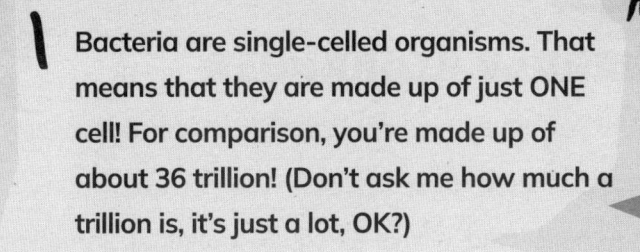

1. Bacteria are single-celled organisms. That means that they are made up of just ONE cell! For comparison, you're made up of about 36 trillion! (Don't ask me how much a trillion is, it's just a lot, OK?)

2. They come in all sorts of shapes and sizes, such as round 'coccus', spiral 'spirilla' and rod-shaped 'bacillus'. Ooh, fancy! You only come in a human shape, how boring!

3. Bacteria are the oldest living things on the planet. They first appeared more than three billion years ago (they are much, much, much, much, much older than your parents, believe it or not).

4. Most bacteria are actually good. For example, there are BILLIONS of bacteria in your belly helping you digest food. Aw, thanks, bacteria.

5. But some are definitely bad and make you ill (boooo, naughty bacteria!), which means we must be on our guard and wash our hands after the loo and before we eat food.

DEADLY DIARRHOEA

One very nasty type of bacteria is called cholera. The disease it causes can give you horrible, watery diarrhoea, which is not very pleasant at all. Sometimes things get so bad and people get so dehydrated (lacking water) that they die! **YIKES!** As well, all that runny diarrhoea coming out of bums is full of pesky bacteria just waiting to pounce, so it's a disease that can be spread super easily. In 1831 there was an outbreak of cholera in London that killed more than **5,000 people**. In 1848 the disease came back again and this time it was even worse – more than **14,000 Londoners died**. In 1853 more than **10,000 died** of the watery diarrhoea disease. **SHEESH!**

People thought what they always did – that the deadly disease was being spread by 'bad air' floating about on the breeze. But one man, Dr John Snow, was going to put them right. Snow began to do some investigating and he noticed that lots of people were getting sick in the same parts of London.

That was odd — breezes don't stay in the same place, so why would the disease? Snow drew up a map of the streets where cholera cases were happening. It quickly became clear from his drawing that they all had something in common.

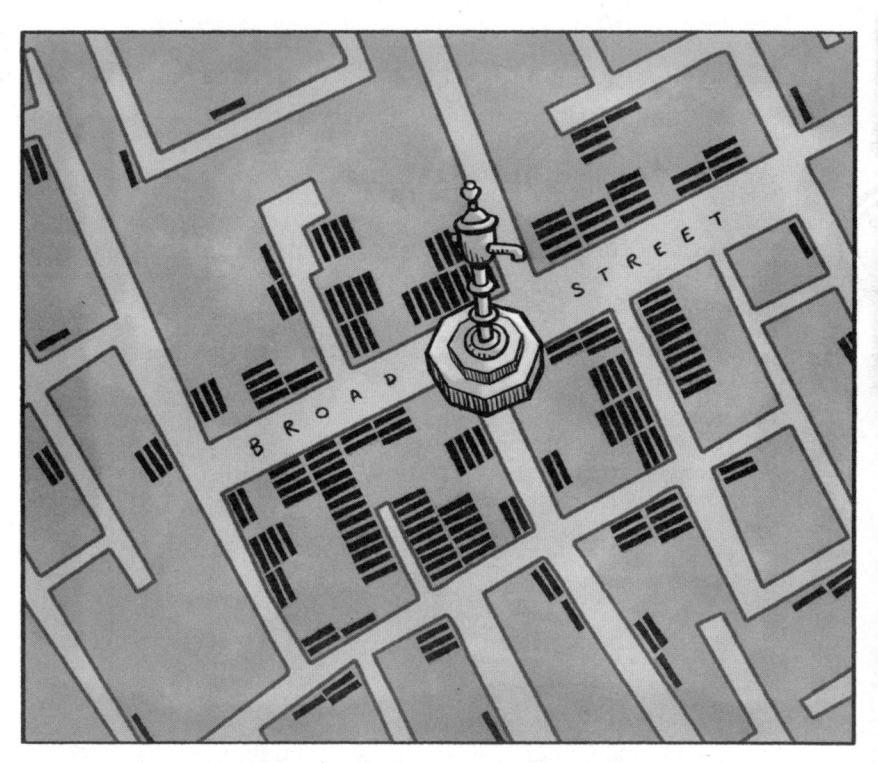

Dr Snow marked each case of cholera on the map with a bar, so it was easy to see where cases were piling up.

131

The people getting sick had been getting their water from water pumps on Broad Street. **That suggested that the disease was being spread in water, NOT in the air, like everyone thought.**

Few people listened to Dr Snow's ideas, thinking they were silly. But guess what? When he took the handle off the pump – stopping people from being able to access the water – fewer people fell ill. **His theory was CORRECT.** It turned out that cesspits underneath the houses on Broad Street were overflowing and poo was leaking into the water. When people took water from the pump to drink, they were being infected by cholera. **Well done science – and Dr Snow – for being on the RIGHT side of history!**

DID YOU HEAR THE JOKE ABOUT THE BACTERIA?

ACTUALLY, NEVER MIND, I DON'T WANT TO SPREAD IT AROUND.

TACKLING TYPHOID

Another disease spread by infected poo getting into food and water supplies is typhoid, which is caused by the bacteria **Salmonella typhi**. When infected, it gives people tummy pain, fevers, tiredness, headaches and sometimes a nasty red rash. Their poo can also get bunged up, or so loose they end up with diarrhoea. Poor things!

Queen Victoria's husband, Prince Albert, is thought to have died of typhoid fever on 14 December 1861, and their eldest son, Bertie, came very close to dying of it too, ten years to the day later. He survived and went on to become King Edward VII.

One famous carrier of typhoid bacteria was a woman called Mary Mallon. Mary worked in a kitchen in New York back in 1907, and while she never got ill herself, she kept passing on typhoid without even knowing about it. This is called being an **asymptomatic carrier**.

DID YOU KNOW?

Asymptomatic carrier = someone who is NOT ill, but passes on a disease

Symptomatic carrier = someone who IS ill and passes on a disease (like when someone sneezes on the bus and it goes all over you – SHUDDER!)

While Mary was cooking food for people, she was accidentally spreading germs to them in their food. Fifty-three people became sick with the disease and three of them died. Three thousand New Yorkers had typhoid when Mary was working in the kitchens and it is thought that she was the source of **ALL of their sickness**.

Mary had to leave her job and she was made to quarantine – **which is a bit like being in lockdown but MUCH more extreme**. This happened to her twice and she was kept alone and away from friends and family for 26 years in total. They tried a lot of treatments on Mary but sadly none of them worked. **Poor Mary!**

In 1964 in the Scottish city of Aberdeen, an outbreak of typhoid caused **407 illnesses and three deaths**. It turned out that a shop in the city was selling corned beef from a tin from Argentina that had traces of poo and *Salmonella* bacteria inside.

The germs were spread to a meat-slicing machine that was then used to slice all sorts of other meats, meaning the disease spread.

GERM THEORY

Eventually, the idea that 'miasma' was behind diseases died out completely. It was replaced by the much more sensible germ theory, which states that some diseases are caused by tiny microbes. These microbes are so teeny tiny that they can only be seen under a microscope. The idea was put forward by French scientist Louis Pasteur. He worked out that you could kill bad bacteria by boiling liquid, such as milk, making it safe to drink. As well as this, he pioneered the first vaccines, which have been keeping people safe from disease ever since.

See ya later, 'bad air' — say hello to amazing science!

CHAPTER TEN: POO AT WAR!

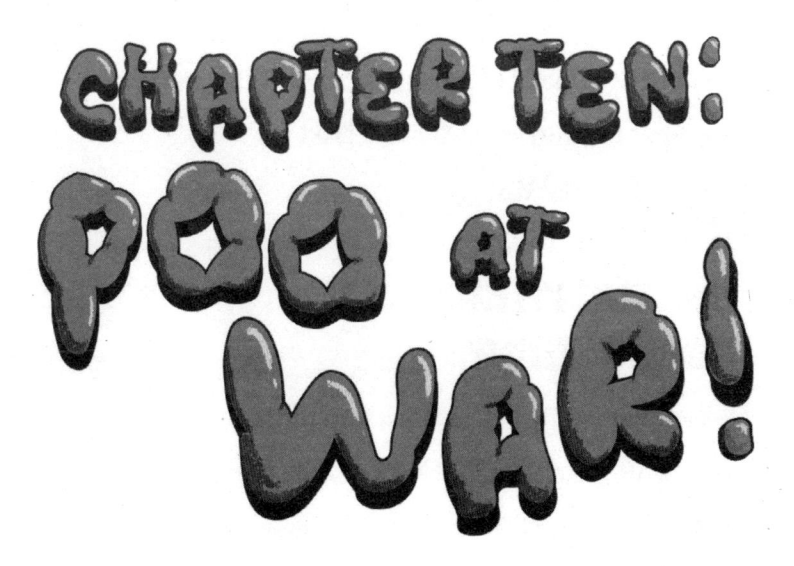

It's not just bombs, bullets and swords flying about everywhere if you go to war – you need to watch out for poo, too! **(Well, maybe not literally – I've never seen a poo gun or a poo sword, have you?)** Over the course of history, thousands upon thousands of soldiers who have gone to war have been killed by poo problems such as diarrhoea.

It's a huge problem for armies. Poor pooing conditions mean that germs can get into water supplies. When a camp of only 10,000 soldiers can produce up to 4 tonnes of poo every single day, that's a problem just waiting to happen! **(4 tonnes is about the weight of a hippopotamus — or should that be a HIPPO-POO-TAMUS?)**

POOING IN EXTREME CONDITIONS

When the French Emperor Napoleon Bonaparte invaded Russia in 1812, it led to a terrible disaster. Not only were lots of citizens killed — so too were his soldiers. As they marched through Russia, thousands were struck down by disease, awful weather and extreme hunger.

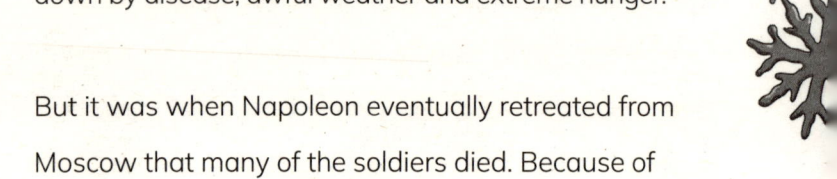

But it was when Napoleon eventually retreated from Moscow that many of the soldiers died. Because of the extremely chilly conditions — which Russia is, erm, known for! — a lot of them got sick. Even worse was when they needed to do a poo. Many found that once they took their trousers down, their fingers were so frozen that they couldn't button them up again! **I don't know about you, but my bum's getting a chill just thinking about it!**

WHAT DO YOU GET IF A SNOWMAN NEEDS A POO?

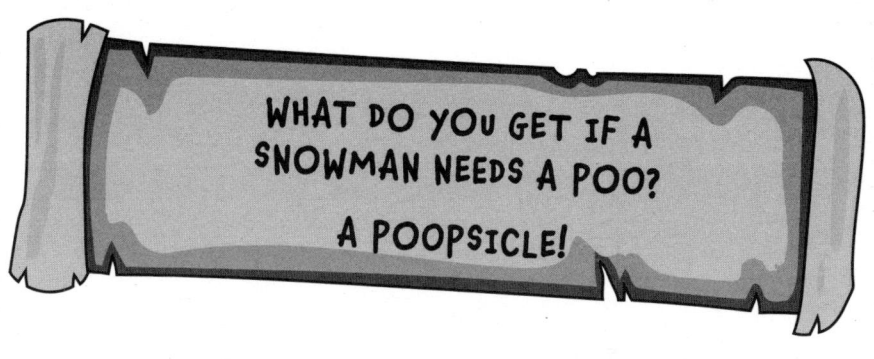

A POOPSICLE!

There's a story told about a British Army officer who was having a terrible time with a sore tummy in 1809, at the Battle of Talavera in Spain. He suddenly needed to do a poo, but he was worried that his men might think he was deserting during the battle if he left. Instead, he ran out in front of the canons, **pulled down his trousers and did his business right there in front of everyone!**

Feeling much better, he did his trousers up again, and his men cheered. Nobody won the battle, but the French did retreat. **Maybe they got a whiff of what the British officer had left and scarpered, quick!**

CRIMEAN WAR

The Crimean War was fought in the 1850s between Russia and the Ottoman Empire, which was supported by France and Britain. It's remembered for lots of things, including the famous Charge of the Light Brigade, when over a hundred British soldiers were killed during a charge towards Russian canons. That happened at the Battle of Balaclava **(which is how balaclavas got their name)** and they were led by Lord Cardigan **(that's where cardigans got their name too!)**. What's with all the knitwear? What next? **Lord Jumper at the Battle of the Woolly Socks?** The Crimean War is also remembered for the work of nurse Florence Nightingale. Nightingale worked hard to keep the soldiers and their hospital clean, in an age when commanders did not recognise the need to worry about sanitation for the soldiers.

> **DID YOU KNOW?**
> During the American Civil War, as many as a massive 95,000 soldiers died of dysentery.

POO PATROLS IN THE TRENCHES OF THE FIRST WORLD WAR

Sixty years after the Crimean War, between 1914 and 1918, even more fighting raged across Europe. This was the First World War. It's also known as the Great War because it was so big and so many people were involved – but trust me, there was nothing 'great' about it. Some people called it The War to End Wars because they couldn't imagine anything bigger or worse. But sadly it wasn't the last war, because us humans just keep fighting.

DID YOU KNOW?

- The First World War was fought between the 'Allies', France, the UK, Russia, Italy, Japan and the USA, against the 'Central' powers of Germany, Austria-Hungary, Bulgaria and Turkey.

- By 1915, the war in Europe had descended into what's known as trench warfare. Hundreds of miles of muddy ditches were carved from Belgium all the way to Switzerland. Soldiers had to live there in terrible conditions and fight each other.

- Powerful new weapons such as artillery guns and huge tanks were all used for the first time.

In the European trenches of the First World War there were no flushing loos. Toilets were known as latrines, and they were **not pleasant AT ALL**. Some latrines were just buckets that could be emptied and cleaned out. Some were simply tree trunks on a frame that soldiers could sit on and let their bum stick out the other side, over a pit. Others were boxes with lids that were kept in rows so that soldiers would sit next to each other to poo, just like the Roman public loos two thousand years before. There were even boxes that looked just like the Tudor close stools that Henry VIII and Elizabeth I used (but definitely no soft cushions and fancy ribbons like they had).

The soldiers were under strict orders not to do their business anywhere but at the latrines. They could get into a lot of trouble from their superiors if they broke the rules – **they didn't want to risk spreading diseases**.

DOING YOUR DUTY

Each company of soldiers had two people whose job was to look after the toilets. These duties were often handed out as punishments to those who had been caught breaking the rules. With so many soldiers in the trenches on both sides, there was always someone who needed to pop to the loo. But latrines were dangerous places. The enemy could aim their fire towards the toilets to catch people with their trousers down! They had to get in and out fast or risk being a target. **Talk about pooing under pressure!**

At night, in the dark, they couldn't use lanterns to guide the way in case it gave away their position. One hapless soldier took a wrong turn one night trying to find the latrine and ended up doing a poo in an officer's sleeping area! **Luckily the officer saw the funny side and he didn't get into trouble. PHEW!**

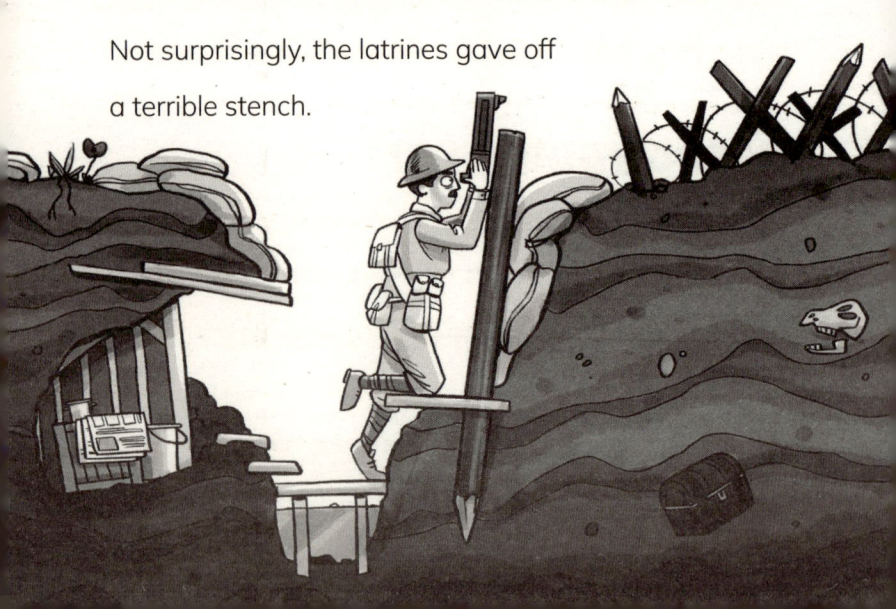

Not surprisingly, the latrines gave off a terrible stench.

There also wasn't much toilet paper going about, either, so they had to make do with whatever they could find to wipe themselves clean. They often used bits of newspaper... **when they'd finished reading it, of course!** Because of the fighting, soldiers couldn't just wander off to use the loo when they felt like it. Instead, they had to use things they had to hand, such as empty tins that had been used to bring biscuits and chopped beef to the front line. Once they were finished, they would empty their poo over the top of the trench, but they kept the tin to use for next time.

BLURGH!

THE GREAT LATRINE ESCAPE OF THE SECOND WORLD WAR

The Second World War came not long after the first, occurring between 1939 and 1945. The Nazi party of Germany, led by Adolf Hitler, had invaded other countries in Europe, and the other countries were fighting back. Once again people were fighting for power in Europe and the world. The fighting was not just on the ground though; there were battles at sea between the navies and there were battles in the sky between the air forces.

DID YOU KNOW?

- The Second World War was fought between the 'Allies', Britain, France, Russia, China and the USA, and the 'Axis' powers of Germany, Italy and Japan. But many other countries were drawn into the conflict too.

- 💩 Germany had been invading countries in Europe, but when they went into Poland, that was the moment the United Kingdom and France declared war.

- 💩 Major battles included the Battle of Britain, the D-Day Landings (France), the Battle of Stalingrad (Russia) and Pearl Harbor (USA).

William Ash was a pilot in the Royal Air Force of Great Britain, where he flew an aeroplane known as the Spitfire. When he was flying over Europe one day, his Spitfire was hit. He survived but was captured by the Germans and sent to a camp for prisoners of war. He tried many times to escape from the camp – one time he tried to tunnel his way out of a latrine! He dived inside, waded through the poo and escaped where it came out the other side. Unfortunately, Ash was captured again – **maybe the Germans could track him down because of the smell!**

THE U-BOAT TOILET DISASTER

Not everyone fighting in the Second World War had a row of latrines to visit. For sailors on board ships it was easy enough; poo could just be thrown overboard. On submarines it was a little more challenging.

In April 1945, just as the war was coming to an end, U-1206, a German submarine, was on a patrol off the coast of Aberdeenshire in Scotland. U-boats, as German submarines were known, were a danger to British ships. They would sneak around underwater and try to sink them! **But that wasn't going to happen with this U-boat, and it was all down to a piece of poo!** U-1206 had some fancy toilet technology on board, but the problem was, Captain Karl-Adolf Schlitt couldn't get it to work. He called on an engineer to come and help flush away a poo he'd left, but the engineer **made a terrible error and**

pulled the wrong lever. These toilets were designed to flush the poop out into the ocean rather than leaving it all inside the boat. But by pulling the wrong lever, **he allowed seawater to flood in.** It mixed with the poo and started to leak on to the ship's batteries. This produced **chlorine gas**, which is **SUPER TOXIC**, so the captain had to bring the boat to the surface.

WHAT A MISTAKE!

When they emerged, it was broad daylight and they were soon spotted by a Royal Air Force patrol, which attacked the boat. The captain ordered the submarine to be sunk so the British couldn't get their hands on it. Four of his men drowned in the choppy North Sea waters and 46 others were captured. What a disaster for Captain Schlitt. **He just wanted to use the toilet!**

HOW TO POO INSIDE A TANK

If you think pooing in a submarine was bad, just imagine what it was like pooing in a tank. They were very small and cramped and there was no privacy at all. One tank commander from New Zealand figured out that empty shell casings left over when the giant bullets were fired could be used to poop into. All you had to do after that was push it out of the little hatches on the tanks and you were done! Just as long as they had cooled down, though, because they get very hot when they're fired – you don't want one of those near your bum! And you'd have to get on very well with the other soldiers in there, too – they'd be able to see, hear and smell everything!

CHAPTER ELEVEN: POO DISCOVERIES

Pooing in wartime is no joke, but neither is pooing down under! A toilet in Australia is sometimes known as a dunny. It comes from the old English word, dunnykin, which means container for dung. **(Well, that makes sense! But why not poopies or ploppies, hmm?)**

Outdoor dunnies aren't just useful for when you want to poop, they also provide temporary homes for all sorts of creatures. People have opened dunnies to be greeted by insects, maggots, frogs, spiders and snakes wriggling about in there. **URGH – why can't we be left to poo in peace?**

As creepy as the prospect of creatures lurking in the loo is, sometimes looking for a toilet can lead to some incredible discoveries from tens or even hundreds of thousands of years ago. **Just wait and see . . .**

SLIPPERY SPIDERS AND FROGS IN BOGS

When it gets warm in Australia, some snakes like nothing better than to sunbathe. **I can't blame them!** And when it's really warm, some like to seek out water. Because snakes are long and thin, they can slither along pipes, go for a swim in sewers, hang about in toilet bowls and simply make themselves at home wherever they fancy.

NOTHING TO SSSEE HERE. JUSSST AN INNOCENT TOILET TISSSUE DISSSSPENSER. OH YESSS, TAKE A SSSEAT.

Harmless snakes tend to be smaller than big venomous ones, so you'd be more likely to find those in the loo. However, there have also been occasions when great big snakes such as anacondas have been found in toilets in Australia and South America! **YIKES!**

> HAVE YOU EVER SMELT A SNAKE'S POOP?
>
> IT SSSSSSTINKS!

You're also likely to find rats down there, swimming around the sewers and running along pipes, occasionally popping up to say hello. As well, in places where there are outdoor dunnies, black widow spiders have been known to creep about. It's a good place for attracting flies, so sometimes they weave their webs inside the toilet bowl!

A bite from a black widow can be anything from painful to downright deadly. If you were unlucky enough to experience one on the loo, first there would be a sharp burning feeling on your bum. Then you'd feel muscle cramps. Then you'd sweat and feel very sick. These feelings are all the body trying to fight off the toxins that the spider's bite left behind in *your* behind.

That's why it's important to check the toilet in Australia and parts of America before pulling your pants down!

Sometimes in Australia people find possums in their toilets, too. At least snakes, possums and rats are big and we can see them easily when we go to the bathroom. Not like those sneaky spiders. In the Southwest USA it is common to see lizards coming through sewer pipes and up into loos.

Honestly, are none of these animals worried about humans coming along and pooping on their heads?

I WAS ONLY LOOKING FOR A TOILET!

Back in 2011, it wasn't just a snake or a spider one Australian man found when he needed to go for a poo. It was HISTORY.

Dr Clifford Coulthard, who was a researcher and elder in the native Adnyamathanha community, was out surveying gorges in an area about 550 km north of the city of Adelaide. When nature called, he ended up stumbling across a remarkable historical site, home to the earliest evidence of Aboriginal settlement.

Dr Coulthard found a small rock shelter with a blackened roof, which he and his colleague recognised as evidence of ancient human activity. (The black roof was probably from a fire.) The area, known as Warratyi, showed that Aboriginal Australians had settled there some 49,000 years ago. That was 10,000 years earlier than historians had previously thought Aboriginal people had been there. **WOW!**

Dr Coulthard didn't just find a black roof, though, he found ancient tools as well. One was a piece of bone that had been sharpened to a point. It was **38,000–40,000 years old** and was believed to be from the leg of an animal, perhaps a yellow-footed rock wallaby (a cute mammal a bit like a small kangaroo). It could have been used as a needle to sew clothes. There were also blade-like tools, which would have been useful for all sorts of things, such as making holes in the hides of animals, which could then be worn as clothes. Dr Coulthard and his team also found evidence of red and white pigments that would have been used for art and body painting.

DID YOU KNOW?

The term Aboriginal refers to people who have inhabited Australia for at least 45,000–50,000 years, possibly more. These people were in Australia WAY before Europeans claimed to have 'discovered' it just a few hundred years ago.

- It is thought that the first Aboriginal people made their way to Australia from Southeast Asia, back when sea levels were much lower.

- Land and the natural world is sacred to the Aboriginal people and is a central part of their heritage and culture.

- Some of the oldest artworks in the world can be found in cave paintings created by Aboriginal artists.

- One of the oldest musical instruments, the didgeridoo, was created by Aboriginal people.

Archaeologists (scientists who study old human history by digging up old sites) also found evidence of humans interacting with giant animals known as megafauna.

Coulthard's colleague Giles Hamm and the excavation team found more than **4,300 artefacts** in total, with **200 bone fragments from 16 mammals and even one reptile**. They also discovered bones from the extinct giant wombat-like *Diprotodon optatum*, and eggs from an ancient giant bird.

The find was very exciting and completely changed what we knew about Aboriginal history, and it was all because Dr Coulthard needed the loo!

TRACKING EXPLORERS WITH POO!

But it's not just needing a poo that alerts archaeologists and historians to history, **it's poo itself**. In 1804 two men called Captain Meriwether Lewis and Lieutenant William Clark set out with thirty-three others on an adventure that would last two years. **Why?** To explore the land and waterways of Northwestern America and find their way to the Pacific Ocean. **And how do we know so much about it? Well, poo, of course.**

They were a hardy bunch, which they had to be, because their journey was fraught with danger. There was risk of injury, disease, animals and insects attacking them and spreading disease.

They were helped by a **remarkable Native American woman** from the Shoshone group, called Sacagawea. She acted as an interpreter, helped with navigation and helped the group find edible plants along the way. Nevertheless, on the long, treacherous trip, stomach bugs were common.

In 1804, some people thought diseases upset the balance of four liquids in the body known as humours. The humours were called black bile, yellow bile, blood and phlegm, and when someone was ill, it was thought that these humours had to be rebalanced.

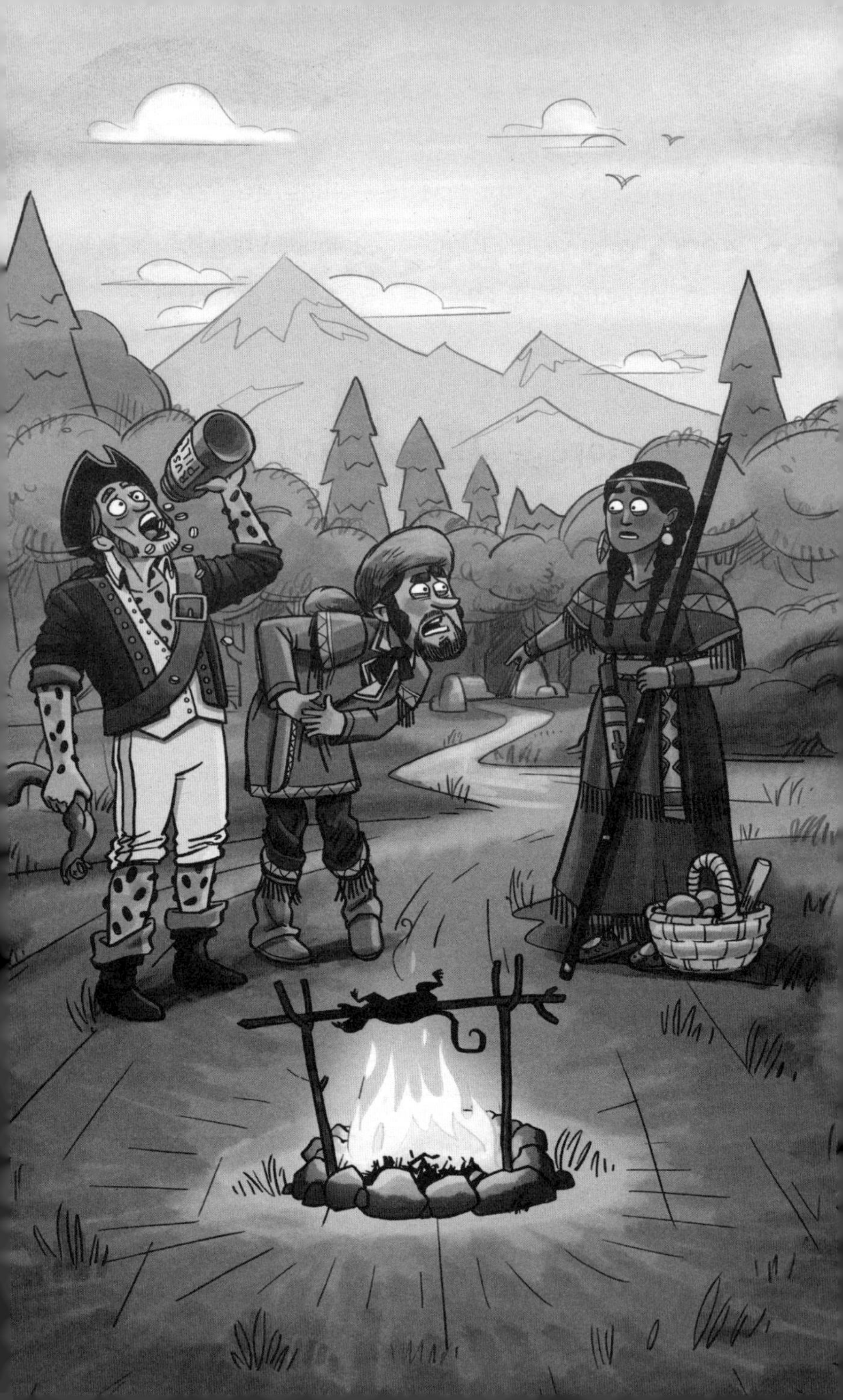

They didn't have to stand on their heads or try to stand on one foot, however; balancing the humours was about removing fluids that they believed were building up inside their bodies.

Much more sensible – NOT!

They removed fluids by taking blood away (sometimes using leeches, which are like blood-sucking slugs) or by making the unwell person be sick on purpose. Another way was to make them have terrible diarrhoea. They did this by giving them a type of medicine called a laxative.

Lewis and Clark carried a supply of laxative pills with them on the expedition because their diet was going to have a lot of meat and not much else. They were called Dr Rush's Bilious Pills, named after the doctor who made them. He really did believe that diarrhoea was the way to treat people who were unwell!

QUICK QUESTION

Dr Rush's pills were also called Thunderclaps because they made the sick patient have to suddenly rush to the toilet without much warning! What would you call yours?

Lightning poopers?

Speedy ploppers?

Poo pushers?

The powerful ingredient in the medicine was mercury, a metal that is very toxic and dangerous to humans. When people on the expedition took pills containing mercury, their bodies would have quickly squeezed the guts hard until all the poo was pushed out. That's why diarrhoea happens – **your body is quickly expelling**

any bad toxins from inside the body before they can do more damage. Diarrhoea can hurt the tummy and is not very nice, but the body does it for good reason, to help us get better.

What was remarkable about it all is that 200 years later, the mercury that came out while the travellers pooped helped historians and archaeologists pinpoint their exact movements.

The researchers found latrine pits at an area called Traveler's Rest where they suspected the expedition might have camped. When they had a good rummage through them **(I hope they wore gloves)** they found high levels of mercury just like the type found in Dr Rush's pills. The mercury had been through the explorers' guts, come out the other end when they rushed to the loo with diarrhoea and then sat there in the pits for 200 years before being found by some curious scientists. It was helpful that mercury does not rot away like other things do.

DISTANT DISCOVERIES

Some poo discoveries go

way,

way,

way back.

Neanderthals were early humans who lived **400,000 to 40,000 years ago**. It used to be thought that they were carnivores who ate mostly meat. But when coprolites (remember, they are fossilised poos) were found, 50,000 years after they had left them behind, they told us a different story. By digging into the ancient coprolites it was found that they were full of vegetable remains too. That made us change our minds about who walked and pooped on the Earth before us.

There are poo discoveries everywhere!

Poo is always telling us about our past . . . but what if it can tell us about the future, too?

CHAPTER TWELVE: POO IN SPACE – AND BEYOND!

We've seen poo and muck and toilet troubles from the ancient Romans and Greeks to medieval kings and queens, Tudors, Victorians and more. **Now it's time for poo to take the ultimate journey and BLAST OFF out of bums and up into space!**

Wherever us humans have been, we've always needed to poo, and with all that poo, we've needed to come up with ways of getting rid of it. In space, that isn't so easy, but astronauts have been flying around up there since 1961, when Russian cosmonaut Yuri Gagarin orbited the Earth aboard the spacecraft Vostok 1.

He was only up in space for 108 minutes, so nobody needed to worry about whether or not he might need to poo. But since then, with longer space journeys, scientists and engineers have had to come up with different ways to keep astronauts and their **spaceships clean and poo-free while they're on their travels!**

ONE SMALL POO FOR MAN . . .

With no gravity in space, poop doesn't just plop down into a toilet bowl like normal. If astronauts didn't have special equipment to help them, **poo would fly around inside spaceships**, hitting them in the head or plopping on to the controls and getting them all mucky. **Not ideal when you're supposed to be exploring the galaxy!**

That's why there are space toilets, which have special seats and tubes that collect poo and pee and work in zero-gravity. Astronauts sit on the seat, just like we do on regular toilets, but instead of the poo falling down, it gets sucked away by air into the tube. Once the poo is collected, it is sealed into a container. **(I hope they put the lid**

on tight!) The containers full of poo are then kept on the spacecraft until it returns to Earth. When the spacecraft comes back, the poo is disposed of properly.

So that's how astronauts take care of their poo in space. It may seem a bit strange, but it's an essential part of living and working when you're not on Earth.

> **WHAT'S SMELLIER THAN THE UNIVERSE?**
>
> **THE POO-NIVERSE!**

POO BAGS

NASA's first long mission was Gemini V. In 1965, American astronauts Gordon Cooper and Pete Conrad spent eight days in orbit around the Earth. They were testing the spacecraft's fuel cells before their planned mission to the Moon. Even though they were given diets designed to produce only small amounts of poop, the two astronauts had to go four times while they were in flight. It was a messy time and they had to figure out how to deal with it all.

They were given a long bag with a small hole at one end surrounded by sticky tape. The sticky tape would stick to their bum to make a good seal. Inside the bag was a chemical that would kill any bacteria and try to stop any smells. **That was an important part because they had to keep the poo on board until they got home!**

Going to the toilet in a bag on a Gemini flight was very tricky and could take up to an hour. The astronauts were closely packed in, like sardines in a little tin. When they needed to go, they had to try to squeeze into a corner, away from the others. They couldn't risk getting any poo on their clothes, because there was no way of washing it off the fabric in the spacecraft, so they had to take them off! Once ready, they would place the sticky, open end of the bag against their bums and go. It wasn't easy, but when you have to go, you have to go.

DID YOU KNOW?

Space travel was BIG in the mid-twentieth century. Amazing advances in technology and engineering meant that humans were able to blast off outside of the Earth's atmosphere for the very first time (taking their poo with them, of course).

- In 1957, Sputnik 1 was the first satellite successfully launched into space, by the Russians (I wonder if it spotted any alien poo up there?).

- The first animal in space was a dog called Laika. Since then, all sorts of

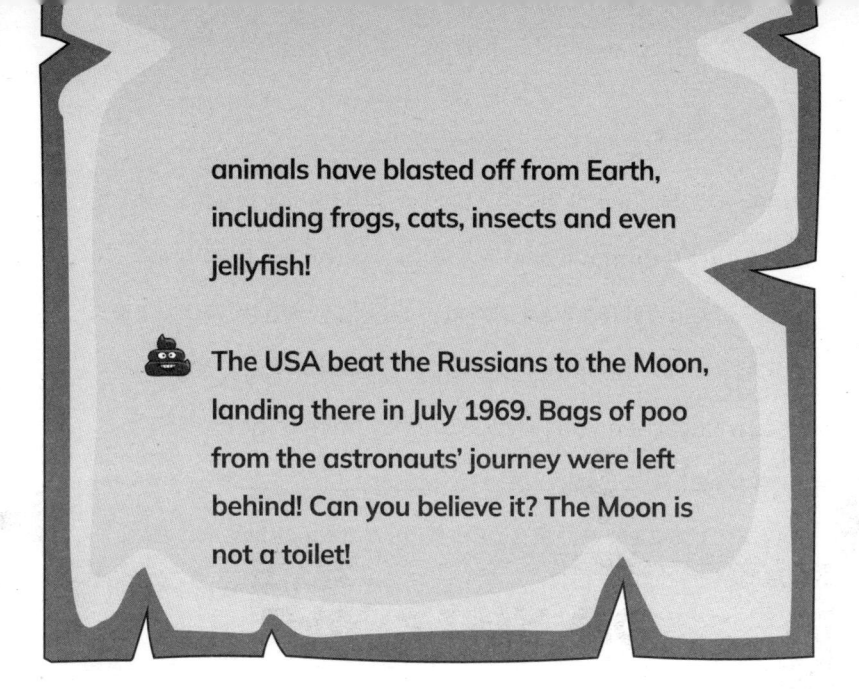

animals have blasted off from Earth, including frogs, cats, insects and even jellyfish!

💩 **The USA beat the Russians to the Moon, landing there in July 1969. Bags of poo from the astronauts' journey were left behind! Can you believe it? The Moon is not a toilet!**

Sometimes pooing in space can go wrong. When NASA's Apollo 10 mission was making its trip back from the Moon, a poo escaped! The astronauts saw it flying past them in the cabin! None of them claimed it to be theirs, though. **'Mine was stickier than that,' one of them said! At least they saw the funny side.**

With the beginning of NASA's Space Shuttle programme came more complicated ways to get rid of the astronauts' poo. Some crews jettisoned (threw out) the waste; others used vacuum bags to take it back to Earth. On the Moon, astronauts couldn't lift their suits like knights in shining armour. They couldn't even use a bag to poop into like they did on the shuttle.

So what did they do? The Moon-landing astronauts wore specially-made pants that were just like nappies. That meant that if they had to go while they were on the Moon, they would do it in their suits and clean it all up later. **(That's why you should always use the toilet before long journeys!)**

All sorts of space programmes have tried all sorts of toilets. A loo used by the Russians cost £15 million! **I bet your toilet didn't cost that much.** This expensive toilet is used on the International Space Station. It collects all the poop in special storage canisters, which are loaded on to a cargo ship that burns up on re-entry through the Earth's atmosphere.

To get further into space and travel further away from Earth, there will have to be more innovative ways for astronauts to deal with their poo, because it won't be possible to store it all inside the spaceships on really long journeys.

QUICK QUESTION

What if astronauts met aliens in space? How would they explain the containers full of poo on board? Maybe the aliens would have their own poo collection too! What would an alien poo even look like? Purple and sparkly? The size of a comet? Maybe it would even be ALIVE!

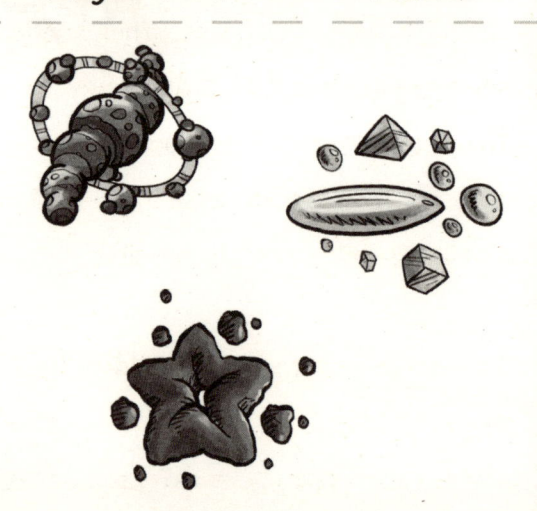

POOS OF THE FUTURE...

There is so much we can learn from all these different eras of history. We can see how people built their toilets, how they cleaned everything up and what they did with all the poo they made. **And boy, was there a lot of it!**

Big cities throughout history thrived when they developed latrines and water-flowing systems to move water and waste about, and to take it away to use elsewhere. When they let it all collect in pits, it caused all sorts of trouble, from overflowing collections to explosions and the spread of diseases. When London built better sewers, it made a **HUGE difference to public health** by stopping the cholera bacteria from spreading so easily. It does make sense that we might want to wash all that as far away as possible.

Although poo might be our waste, **it shouldn't be wasted!** Nothing was wasted in the ancient cities and the poo was used as fertiliser to grow crops. From the

poo canoes of the Aztecs taking away the nutrient-rich dung to spread on the crops of the floating gardens, to the medieval gong farmers taking away buckets of poop at night, people have in the past been paid well to provide a useful service. Today we press a button and flush poop away to end up pumped into the sea.
What a waste!

It used to be that we would pull a chain or a handle to flush our toilets, but some toilets have buttons now. And not just one button but two.

The dual-flush system was designed for places where water is scarce, but it has been adopted around the world, to avoid large amounts of fresh water being flushed away into the sewers every time a toilet is used. The bigger flush is for poos, the smaller one for pees.

DID YOU KNOW?

- On average a full flush in a dual-flush toilet can use 6–7 litres of water

- A smaller flush will use 3–4 litres of water

- Old single-flush toilets can use between 13 and 26 litres of water!

It you add it all together, it makes a huge difference to the amount of water being used. What a saving that makes!

In some countries there are aid programmes that allow people to collect their poo and have it turned into fertile soil. An aid programme in Haiti allows them to use their own waste as fertiliser rather than paying lots of money to other countries to ship in chemical fertilisers. The process only takes six months and saves a lot of money and helps the environment.

What a great idea!

Many places where people are concerned for their local environment (such as national parks) are installing composting toilets for visitors to use. **These toilets are dry.** They don't use any water to flush anything away and by adding organic matter such as sawdust and good bacteria to the mix, they break down the poo and turn it into compost. **It's another great way to conserve water and not waste our waste** – so perhaps our medieval friends pooing on straw were on to something! This might be a good idea for places where water is harder to come by, rather than just flushing water away.

If the poo is flushed away and ends up in the sewage system then the gases that we've heard so much about could be **put to good use**. The sludgy mixture of poo and water that ends up in sewage treatment facilities could have bacteria added to make even more gases. These could be used to power houses, schools, factories and vehicles.

For as long as humans have been living on the Earth **(which has been a very long time)** we have had to find ways to deal with all the poo we've made. Sometimes poo was useful, sometimes poo got in the way and sometimes poo made a great big stink. Because we need to wash away our stinky, germ-filled poo, we have come up with all sorts of ingenious inventions to get rid of it. From simple holes in the ground to grand flushing toilets, lots of evidence has been left behind that shows us how our ancestors lived their lives and how they built communities around dealing with their poo waste. **Isn't that poo-tastic?**

So now you know all about poo through the ages and poo in the future, too. I bet you need to go for a poo yourself! Just be grateful for the fantastic piece of technology you sit on – the humble loo. And remember to **WASH YOUR HANDS!**

POO QUIZ

Do you know you poo from your poop? Your dung from your doo-doo?

Well, I hope you've been paying attention, because now it's time to test everything you know about poo through the ages!

Can you tell which of these historical poo facts are true or false? The answers can all be found somewhere in this book – and also hidden away on pages 185-187.

1. Aztecs in the city of Tenochtitlan took their poo away on canoes on their lake.

   TRUE   FALSE

2. Gut worms such as whipworms and maw-worms are parasites can grow up to 2 meters long.

   TRUE   FALSE

3. Poo's brown colour is given to it by brown food such as chocolate and gravy all mushed together.

   TRUE   FALSE

4. During the American Civil War, as many as 95,000 soldiers died of diarrhoea diseases.

   TRUE   FALSE

5. Romans used special stones called *pessoi* to wipe their bums.

TRUE   FALSE

6. The name given to a fossilised piece of poo is a ploprolite.

TRUE   FALSE

7. Bacteria come in lots of different shapes and sizes, including round, spiral and rod-shaped.

TRUE   FALSE

8. The person who looked after Henry VIII's toilet habits was known as Ye Olde Poo Whisperer.

TRUE   FALSE

9. The Erfurt Latrine Disaster was when sixty nobles from the Holy Roman Empire fell into a giant pit full of horse dung.

TRUE   FALSE

10. A garderobe was a special kind of toilet, built on to the side of Medieval castles.

TRUE   FALSE

POO QUIZ ANSWERS

1. TRUE

The poo was transported to fields where it was used as fertiliser to help crops grow.

2. TRUE

They like nothing better than hiding out in people's guts (like the Vikings of days gone by), waiting for the moment to pop their heads out of their bums!

3. FALSE

Poo's brown colour is actually down to dead blood cells that your body gets rid of at the same time as food waste.

4. TRUE

It was one of the leading causes of mortality during the war.

5. FALSE

Romans used special sponges on sticks, called a *xylospongium* or *tersorium*. It was the ancient Greeks who used *pessoi*, of course!

6. FALSE

It's actually a coprolite.

7. TRUE

Sadly bacteria DON'T come shaped like a poo.

8. FALSE

He was actually known as the Groom of the Stool. But honestly, I think Poo Whisperer is better, don't you?

9. FALSE

They actually fell into a giant pit full of HUMAN dung. BLURGH!

10. TRUE

Just remember to watch where you walk if you live in a castle – you never know what might land on your head!

GLOSSARY

If you need help remembering some of the poo-tastic words featured in this book, you can find them here.

Archaeologists are people who study human history and prehistory, by examining physical remains of things found in the ground.

Bacteria are single-celled organisms found almost everywhere on Earth. They can be harmless or harmful – some of the nastier ones include *Salmonella*, *Shigella* and *Escherichia coli*.

Cesspits are holes in the ground where poo is stored.

A **commode** is a seat with a hole and a bowl that we can sit on to poo.

Constipation is when we get bunged up and can't poo. It can make our tummies sore.

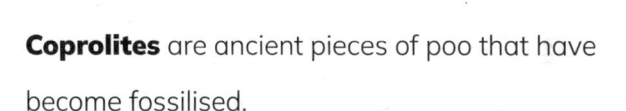

Coprolites are ancient pieces of poo that have become fossilised.

Diarrhoea is when we poo more often than normal and it is runny and smelly.

Excavations are when archaeologists dig into the ground to find evidence of people who lived there in the past.

Fertiliser is spread on fields and gardens to make crops grow. It can be made from poo.

Garderobes are small rooms that are toilets built on to the side of castle and abbey walls.

Medieval times, also known as the Middle Ages, was the period between the fifth and fifteenth centuries.

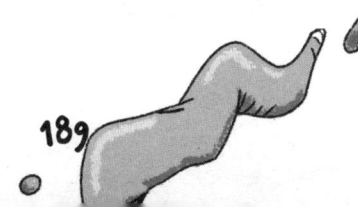

The **Minotaur** was a monster from Greek mythology from the island of Crete. It was half man and half bull. It lived in a labyrinth and was very dangerous. It still had to poo though, just like us.

Parasites are little creatures that live on or in other bodies.

Physicians are doctors who used medicines to treat internal problems.

Poo is the solid waste excreted by the body. It is also known as poop, plop, dung, gong, faeces, excrement and many more wonderful words too.

Quarantine is when people are kept apart from others for a time so they can't pass on infections.

Toilets are handy inventions we use to sit on to do poos! They are also known as loos, latrines, thunderboxes, crappers, jakes, johns and many more names too.

ACKNOWLEDGEMENTS

I would like to thank the team at Wren & Rook, especially Jonny Leighton for his endless patience and humour and Luke Newell for his hilarious illustrations.

Thank you to Emily Glenister and the team at DHH Literary Agency.

And a big thank you to Kathryn and Charlie Edge for still laughing at their mum's silly jokes.

LOOK OUT FOR BOOK 2 IN THE

HISTORY STINKS

SERIES:

WEE, SNOT AND SLIME THROUGH TIME!